RONIN
SKIRMISH WARGAMES
IN THE AGE OF THE SAMURAI

CRAIG WOODFIELD

First published in Great Britain in 2013 by Osprey Publishing,
Midland House, West Way, Botley, Oxford, OX2 0PH, UK
43-01 21st Street, Suite 220B, Long Island City, NY 11101, USA
E-mail: info@ospreypublishing.com

Osprey Publishing is part of the Osprey Group

A CIP catalogue record for this book is available from the British Library

Craig Woodfield has asserted his right under the Copyright, Designs and Patents
Act, 1988, to be identified as the author of this book.

Print ISBN: 978 1 78096 846 9
PDF e-book ISBN: 978 1 78096 847 6
EPUB e-book ISBN: 978 1 78096 848 3

Typeset in Sabon and Myriad Pro
Originated by PDQ Media, Bungay, UK
Printed in China through Worldprint Ltd.

13 14 15 16 17 10 9 8 7 6 5 4 3 2 1

www.ospreypublishing.com

Osprey Publishing is supporting the Woodland Trust, the UK's leading woodland
conservation charity, by funding the dedication of trees.

ACKNOWLEDGEMENTS

Thanks to all that contributed to these rules, particularly Bern Entriken and
Peter West, as well as Phil and all at Osprey Publishing.

Monk miniatures designed by Steve Saleh and painted by Dave Woodward.
Bandits designed by Steve Saleh and painted by Kev Dallimore. Samurai and
Ashigaru figures are by Wargames Factory, painted by Kev Dallimore.
All terrain used in the photographs is the property of Paul Baker and Steve
McGuire. The photo on page 59 is of Bac Ninh Miniatures' Boshin War
command group, painted by Jose Antonio Carmena. Many thanks to all those
involved in the production, preparation and photography of the miniatures.

CONTENTS

INTRODUCTION   **4**
What You Need To Play *Ronin*   4
Models   4
Basic Principles   4

BACKGROUND   **5**
A Time Of War   5
Weapons And Armour   5

GAMEPLAY   **8**
Turn Sequence   8
Priority Phase   8
Move Phase   10
Combat Phase   14
Action Phase   21
End Phase   22

SPECIAL RULES   **22**
Banners   22
Mounted Models   23
Attributes   24

FACTIONS   **26**
Bushi   27
Ikko-Ikki   29
Sohei   31
Koryu   33
Bandits   36
Koreans   38
Ming Chinese   40
Peasants   42
Swords-For-Hire   42
A Sample Buntai   44

SCENARIOS   **45**
Setting Up The Game   45
Skirmish   48
Capture   48
Duel   49
Defence   50
Assassination   51
Tournament   52
Defend The Village   53

CAMPAIGNS   **54**
Progression   54

TOURNAMENTS   **55**

ADVANCED RULES   **56**
Fatigue   57

APPENDIX – OTHER PERIODS   **57**
Kamakura Period   57
Late Edo Period   58

FURTHER READING   **61**
Recommended Reading   61
Films   61

COUNTERS SHEET   **61**

REFERENCE SHEET   **62**

BUNTAI ROSTER   **64**

INTRODUCTION

Ronin is a small-scale skirmish game set in late 16th-century Japan in which small groups of warriors referred to as Buntai fight each other for honour or riches. Rather than just rolling a few dice, *Ronin* allows players to make tactical decisions about how the models that they control will fight – offensively, defensively, or applying special martial skills.

WHAT YOU NEED TO PLAY *RONIN*
- A Buntai of at least 4 and up to 20 models.
- A table and a few pieces of scenery.
- A tape measure and a handful of six-sided dice (referred to as d6).
- About a dozen counters or tokens for each player in two distinct colours, shapes, or sizes.
- Markers to represent wounds (a total of 3 different types) and slain warriors.

MODELS
These rules were designed and play-tested using 28 mm scale miniatures based on 25mm round bases that are referred to through these rules as Models. In *Ronin*, each model has the following Characteristics:

Name and Type – this describes the type of model.

Rank – the relative importance of the model:
- Rank 0 models are peasants and other civilian types with little combat ability.
- Rank 1 and 2 models are basic foot soldiers, well-trained and well-equipped.
- Rank 3 and 4 models are elite warriors with excellent training and equipment.
- Rank 5 models are the best of the best.

Combat Pool – the capacity of the model to make attacks in hand-to-hand combat, as well as defend itself. Rank 0 and 1 models only have a combat pool of 1, Rank 2 have a combat pool of 2, Ranks 3 and 4 have a Combat Pool of 3 and 4 respectively, whilst Rank 5 models have a Combat Pool of 5.

Initiative – the ability of the model to strike quickly, which will often be modified by the type of weapon it is wielding.

Fight – the model's skill with hand-to-hand weapons, ranging from 1 to 5.

Shoot – the model's skill with missile weapons, usually 1.

Armour – the type of armour the model is wearing (if any).

Weapons – the weapons carried by the model.

Attributes – special skills and abilities that the model has.

Points – the cost of the model when building your Buntai.

BASIC PRINCIPLES
The following basic principles are applied when playing *Ronin*.

Measurement – any player is allowed to measure any distance at any time.

Reduced movement – a number of factors reduce the movement of models, but this can never fall below 1".

Reduced Characteristics – a number of factors will reduce models'

Characteristics such as Fight and Initiative. Characteristics can be reduced to 0, but cannot be negative.

D6 rule – when in doubt or disagreement over a particular situation or rule, roll a d6 to determine which interpretation to use.

Facing – models do not have facing in *Ronin*, so models are not disadvantaged or affected by things that happen 'behind' them. Similarly, a model can be rotated on the spot at any time and any number of times, and this does not count as movement.

BACKGROUND

A TIME OF WAR

Ronin is set in the late 16th century near the end of the *Sengoku Jidai* or 'Age of Warring States' period, when feudal lords called Daimyos battled for control of Japan, fighting countless wars and skirmishes against each other. The Emperor of Japan had long been an impotent figurehead and true power was held by the Shogun, the greatest of the Daimyos.

It was during this time the elite warriors known as Samurai reached the peak of their martial abilities. The constant warfare against other Samurai, warrior monks, bandits and pirates produced a class of warrior that was devoted to warfare. Even as Japan was slowly unified under first Oda Nobunaga and then Toyotomi Hideyoshi, the Samurai armies were re-deployed to Korea in a long and ultimately futile war of conquest against the Koreans and their Ming Chinese allies.

WEAPONS AND ARMOUR

The weapons and armour of 16th-century Japan were diverse and complex. This section briefly explains the more common sorts used in these rules.

WEAPONS

Katana: The katana has become one the most famous weapons in history and is commonly known as the Samurai sword. Renowned for its cutting ability, the effectiveness of the katana is a result of its design, construction and the skill of the swordsmen that used it. A typical katana would have a blade length of 60–75cm. The single-edged, concave blade was usually wielded with two hands, but was still effective when used one-handed. Japanese swordmakers perfected a technique of wrapping an incredibly strong but brittle layer of steel around a softer, more flexible one, creating a resilient and versatile weapon. In these rules 'katana' is used as a generic term to describe all Japanese 'long' swords, though this is not strictly correct.

Wakizashi: This smaller sword was often worn paired with a katana (known as daisho), particularly by Samurai.

Tanto: A dagger

Nodachi: The nodachi was a true two-handed sword, with a blade of up to 120 cm long. It was worn across the back and presented its wielder with many problems, not least how to draw it! It was, however, capable of delivering a devastating cut and was originally designed to be used against cavalry.

Naginata: The polearm known as the naginata was the principal weapon of the Sohei warrior monks and also of many Samurai. It consisted of a long, curved blade on a pole up to two metres long. The length of the shaft gave the wielder a distinct advantage against swordsmen, and the curved blade could be used to deliver devastating blows.

Yari: The yari is a spear, functionally identical to those used by almost all warrior cultures throughout history.

Nagae-yari: This is a very long spear or pike, which provided great reach but was very clumsy at close quarters.

Ashigaru defeat a Samurai, by Angus McBride © Osprey Publishing Ltd. Taken from Elite 23: *The Samurai.*

Kasurigama: This unusual weapon consisted of a weight on a long chain attached to a short sickle. Fiendishly hard to master, the weight could be used to entangle or disarm an opponent before he was finished off with the blade.

Tetsubo: This ponderous weapon was a heavy, iron-studded club that required great strength to use.

Jo: The jo was a short staff a little more than 4 feet long. It was developed as a counter to the katana.

Bo: The long staff, or bo, was the height of a man.

Yumi: The Japanese bow was asymmetrical and came in a variety of sizes, but for the purposes of these rules all yumi are considered to be identical in strength and range.

Teppo: The matchlock arquebus known as the teppo was introduced to Japan by Portuguese traders in 1543 and was rapidly adopted by the Samurai. Although it never completely replaced the yumi, its major shortcomings were more than compensated for by its relative ease of use and devastating stopping ability.

Shuriken: The shuriken, or throwing star, was a short ranged missile weapon used by the spies and assassins known as Ninja.

ARMOUR

Japanese armour was ornate and highly complex, with many specialist pieces. Sections were often laced together and lacquered, and bright colours were common. Generally speaking, the more ornate and complex the armour, the more important the individual wearing it. As firearms became more common, some high-ranking Samurai began to wear European-style iron cuirasses or helmets.

Some of the major components of Japanese armour:

Do: Cuirass

Kusazuri: Tassets hanging over the thighs

Sode: Shoulder guards

Kote: Gauntlets

Nodowa: Throat protector

Mempo: Facemask, often ornate with snarling visages and even horsehair moustaches!

Kabuto: Helmet

Jingasa: A conical helmet typical of the Ashigaru

In *Ronin*, the following classes of armour are used:

- Light: A model armoured in this way wears only two or three pieces of armour, perhaps designed to protect his usual fighting aspect or perhaps because it is all that he owns! A bandit or down-on-his-luck ronin may be equipped with light armour.
- Medium: A model wearing medium armour has most of his body well protected, e.g. an Ashigaru or Sohei.
- Heavy: A model wearing heavy armour is likely to be a Samurai or similar high-class warrior, with virtually every part of his body protected.

GAMEPLAY

TURN SEQUENCE

A game of *Ronin* consists of a number of turns, each representing a few seconds of actual time. Each turn is further divided into five phases, shown below in the order in which they are undertaken. Generally, play will alternate between players in each phase (beginning with the player with Priority), but in some phases actions are simultaneous.

1. Priority Phase
2. Move Phase
3. Combat Phase
4. Action Phase
5. End Phase

PRIORITY PHASE

The player who will have Priority for the rest of this turn is determined in this phase. The Morale level of each Buntai is also checked if casualties were suffered in the previous turn or if certain other conditions have been met.

MOVE PHASE

During this phase players have the opportunity to move models or use missile weapons.

COMBAT PHASE

In this phase all hand-to-hand combat is resolved.

ACTION PHASE

During this phase models will have the opportunity to use missile weapons again as well as undertake certain special actions.

END PHASE

In the final part of the turn, some tidying up occurs and Victory Conditions are checked.

PRIORITY PHASE

During the Priority Phase, the player with Priority is determined and then Morale is tested.

1. DETERMINE PRIORITY

Each player rolls a d6 (re-rolling ties). The winner has Priority for this turn. The player with Priority will have the opportunity to choose which combats are resolved first and which models move or fire first. In any situation where there is an opportunity for more than one model to do something, the player with Priority will always have the option to go first.

2. TEST MORALE

Combat is a frightening experience, and despite the best of plans of commanders, warriors will often lose the will to fight. In *Ronin*, this is simulated by the Morale of a Buntai. There are three levels of Morale – Steady, Wavering and Routing. A Buntai will always start a battle with

Morale at Steady. However, if members of the Buntai are killed then its Morale may move to Wavering or even Routing.

You must to check to see if your Buntai's Morale has changed if at least one of the following conditions applies:

- The Buntai's Morale is currently Wavering.
- At least 25% of the starting strength of the Buntai suffered a Critical wound in the previous turn (for example, if a Buntai that started the game with 10 models loses 3 to critical wounds in any one turn, it must test the following turn).
- The Leader of the Buntai suffered a Critical wound in the previous turn.

To test Morale, roll 2d6 and add the two dice together. The resulting number is the Morale Test. Compare this to the Buntai's Morale Rating (which can be found in the special rules for each faction). If the Morale Test is equal to or less than the Morale Rating of the faction, then one of the following will happen:

- If the Buntai's Morale is currently Steady, then nothing will happen.
- If the Buntai's Morale is currently Wavering, it will change to Steady.

If the Morale Test exceeds the Buntai's Morale Rating, then there will be one of two effects:

- If the Buntai's Morale is currently Steady, it will change to Wavering.
- If the Buntai's Morale is currently Wavering, it will change to Routing.

Once a Buntai's Morale changes to Routing, it will remain so for the rest of the game.

Certain conditions will add modifiers to this Morale Test:

- The Buntai is at less than half strength: +1
- The Buntai's Morale is currently Wavering: +1
- The Buntai has at least one model with the Commander ability: -1
- The Buntai has a banner: you may choose to reroll the Morale Test

In any case, a natural Morale Test of 2 (you roll two 1s) is always a success and a natural roll of 12 (two 6s) is always a failure.

WAVERING

When a Buntai's Morale changes from Steady to Wavering, it is beginning to lose the will to fight. Warriors become uncertain and unwilling to risk their lives. Each time that you activate a model in order to move it into base-to-base contact with an enemy model, roll a d6 and add that model's Rank. If the result is 7 or more, then you may move the model. Otherwise, the model may not move into contact, though it may take other actions.

ROUTING

When a Buntai's morale moves to Routing, it begins to withdraw from the battlefield. Each time you activate a model, roll a d6 and add that model's Rank. If the result is 7 or more, the model may act as you wish. Otherwise, it must make a Run or Gallop move towards the nearest table edge, avoiding any enemy models as it moves. If it leaves the table it may not return. Models that are engaged are not affected. Once a Buntai is Routing, it stays that way for the remainder of the game.

MOVE PHASE

During this phase models move or use missile weapons. The player with Priority selects a model to move or use a missile weapon, resolves this, then the other player selects a model, and so on. Once a player passes on the opportunity to move or use a missile weapon, the phase ends for that player.

1. MOVEMENT

The distance a model moves depends on a number of factors, detailed below. Under normal circumstances, models may never move over or through other models, and there must always be room for the model's base where it stops. However, models may move in any direction and may make any number of turns as part of their movement.

A model may normally move up to 6", which may take it into base-to-base contact with an enemy model.

A model may make a Run move of up to 9" if it does not pass within 1" of an enemy model during any part of its movement.

A model's movement is halved if it meets any of the following criteria:

- The model is Stunned or has a Grievous wound.
- The model is Encumbered.
- The model moves through Difficult terrain (see below).

A model may not move if it has used a missile weapon in this phase or is engaged in combat, except to Withdraw.

WITHDRAW

A model that is in base-to-base contact with one or more enemy models may move up to 2" out of contact. The enemy model (or models) has three options in this situation:

1. The enemy model(s) may choose to not move and make a single attack against the departing model. This happens just like a normal attack, but without any opportunities for Enhancing. Additionally, the attacking model gets an additional +1 to its Attack Roll.
2. Do nothing.
3. Move back into base-to-base contact as that model's activation.

TERRAIN

Terrain affects the way models move on the tabletop, and provides cover and concealment. There are four main types of terrain: Difficult, Impassable, Buildings and Water. Before starting the game, it is important that both players discuss the terrain that is to be used and what game effects that it will have in terms of movement and cover (see below).

Difficult terrain: Difficult terrain is that which requires some effort to travel through. Examples include rice paddies, shallow streams and ponds, very rocky ground, thick mud or thick underbrush. Forests do not generally count as difficult ground unless also associated with thick underbrush, and neither do shallow streams. Low walls and fences and similar man-made obstacles will count as difficult terrain. If a model starts its movement in difficult terrain, finishes its movement in difficult terrain or at any point during its movement passes through difficult terrain, its movement will be reduced by half. This stacks with effects detailed above, so if a model is Stunned AND in Difficult Terrain, it will only move 1.5".

Impassable terrain: Impassable terrain includes walls too high to easily climb, cliffs, deep water and so on. Models cannot move through this terrain, they must move around it.

Buildings: Buildings are a special type of terrain and can cause some issues if the rules are not carefully discussed before the start of a game. Because they are easy to defend, generally only one model will be able to attack any enemy model standing in a doorway or window. Many Japanese buildings of this time had light internal walls that could easily be broken through. If agreed to prior to the game, models may move through internal walls as if they were passing through Difficult Terrain.

Models armed with long handled weapons (including yari, nagae-yari, tetsubo, nodachi and naginata) suffer a -1 Initiative penalty and -1 penalty to Attack Rolls when fighting inside buildings, unless the combat is taking place in a very large room.

Water: The effects of water also deserve special attention. A model that is in water that counts as Difficult terrain may drown if it received any Stunned counters. In this situation, a roll of 6 on a d6 results in the model drowning (a type of Critical wound) and being removed as a casualty. If the model is wearing heavy armour, a roll of 5 or 6 gives this result.

2. USE A MISSILE WEAPON

This is the first of two opportunities to use a missile weapon during a turn, the second being in the Action Phase. Using a missile weapon in this turn is considered to be a hurried shot, perhaps at a moving target, and so incurs a penalty to hit. However, models armed with bows will be able to fire up to twice per turn, albeit with reduced effectiveness.

Any model that is not Stunned and not engaged may use a missile weapon in this phase. Using a missile weapon is undertaken slightly differently to hand-to-hand combat, with only the attacker rolling dice.

SHOOTING PROCEDURE

1. Select a target model, and then measure range (from the edge of one base to the edge of the target's) and check line of sight.
2. The model that is shooting rolls 2d6, adds its Shoot Characteristic and then adds or subtracts other modifiers due to the range and/or weather conditions. This is the Shooting Attack Roll.
3. The base Shooting Defence Score is 6 for all models, and the target adds any modifiers due to armour or cover to this value.
4. Subtract the final Shooting Defence Score from the Shooting Attack Roll. The resulting number is the Wound Score. If the Wound Score is 1 or more, then a wound may have been caused. Refer to the Wound Table (page 19). If the Wound Score is negative or 0, the attack has failed.

Modifiers to Shooting Attack Roll	
Target is less than 6" away	+1
Target is 12–24" away	-1
Target is 24–36" away	-2 (-3 if shooting with a teppo)
Target is more than 36" away	-3 (-4 if shooting with a teppo)
Target is engaged in combat	-1 (plus see special rules for shooting into combat)
Shooting Model made a normal move this turn	-1
Shooting Model made a Run or Gallop move this turn	-2
Shooting Model previously fired this turn	-1
Shooting Model is shooting in the Move Phase	-1
Shooting Model has a Grievous wound	-1
All modifiers are cumulative.	

Modifiers to Shooting Defence Score	
Target has light armour	+1
Target has medium armour	+2
Target has heavy armour	+3
Target is in Light cover	+1
Target is in Heavy cover	+2
All modifiers are cumulative.	

LINE OF SIGHT AND COVER

Certain types of terrain will offer cover to models that are targeted by Shooting Attacks. There are two types of cover – Light and Heavy. Light cover includes vegetation such as shrubs and hedges, which obscure the target and offer minor protection. Models benefitting from Light cover gain a +1 benefit to their Defence Score. Heavy cover includes walls, building, embankments, wooden palisades and so on, and provides a +2 bonus to the Defence Score.

Line of sight is the ability of a model to see a target. If there is no line of sight, an attack may not be made. The following situations block line of sight:

- If a straight line between any part of the attacker's base to any part of the target's base crosses any part of the base of another model.
- If there is more than 2" of Light cover in between the model and the target.
- If there is any amount of Heavy cover AND the target model has not moved or used a missile weapon this turn.

MISSILE WEAPONS

Weapon	Maximum Range	Wound Modifier	Special
Shuriken (throwing star)	6″	-2	There is no penalty for moving and using a shuriken.
Teppo (arquebus)	48″	Special	The teppo, or arquebus, must be reloaded before it can be fired again (see Action Phase, below). Whenever a teppo is fired, it is helpful to place a small ball of cotton wool or similar next to the model to signify this. A teppo is inaccurate at long ranges, and so all shots of more than 24″ incur an additional -1 penalty. Models that are fired at with a teppo do not gain any benefits from light or medium armour, and heavy armour is considered to be light armour.
Yumi (bow)	48″		

SHOOTING INTO COMBAT

Sometimes you will elect to shoot at a model already engaged in combat. This is a risky proposition, and if the shot misses it may hit one of the other combatants. The usual process is followed, but if the Shooting Attack is a failure, randomly select another model in the combat and conduct a completely new Shooting Attack against that model, including a new dice roll. This represents the initial shot missing the target model but potentially hitting a second model. If this second attack fails, then the shot was a failure – do not continue for a third model in the combat (if one exists).

SHOOTING EXAMPLE

An Ashigaru with a yumi decides to shoot at a Samurai during the Move Phase. The Ashigaru hasn't moved and can draw a clear line of sight to the Samurai, so is eligible to shoot at him. He rolls 2d6, getting a 7, and adds his Shoot Characteristic of 1. Because the Samurai is 14″ away, he subtracts 1 from this score and, finally, he subtracts an additional 1 for shooting in the Move Phase. His final Shooting Attack Roll is 6.

The Samurai's basic Shooting Defence Score is 6 (as it is for all models). He adds 3 for his heavy armour giving him a final Shooting Defence Score of 9. Subtracting the Samurai's Shooting Defence Score of 9 from the Ashigaru's Shooting Attack Roll of 6 gives a Wound Score of -3, so no wound results.

Later in that turn, during the Action Phase, the Ashigaru decides to shoot again at the Samurai, who has since closed to just 5" – worryingly close. This time the Ashigaru rolls 10 on 2d6, and again adds his Shooting Characteristic of 1. Because the Samurai is less than 6" away he gets a +1 modifier, but because he has already shot once this turn, there is an additional -1 modifier. This time his final Shooting Attack Roll is 11.

As before, the Samurai's Defence score is 9. Subtracting this from the Ashigaru's final Shooting Attack Roll of 11 gives a Wound Score of 2. Consulting the Wound Table, this means that the Samurai has suffered a Light wound. But will this be enough to save the plucky Ashigaru archer?

COMBAT PHASE

During this phase models that are engaged fight in hand-to-hand combat.

The key mechanic for resolving combat in *Ronin* is the use of Attack and Defence Counters, which are drawn from the relevant model's Combat Pool. We recommend using black and white stones such as those used in the Japanese strategy game Go, but any sort of counter that comes in two clearly distinguishable colours, shapes or sizes can be used. Before starting the game, make sure that each player is clear about which counters are which! Each player should have a pool of around half a dozen of each colour, perhaps stored in a small bowl or container. Each combat will have a number of opportunities for attack or defence by each of the models involved in the combat. It is not compulsory, however, for any attacks to be made and indeed an entire combat round may pass without this happening.

All models that are in base-to-base contact with one or more enemy models are considered to be engaged in hand-to-hand combat. Up to four models may fight against a single model – models in excess of this make no contribution to the combat.

Sometimes more than one model from each side will become involved in a single combat. In this case, the models should be separated into a logical number of separate combats, depending on the sequence in which they joined the combat and which models are in base-to-base contact with which. Common sense needs to be applied in these situations, and the golden rule is that only ONE side will ever have multiple combatants in any given combat.

The player with Priority picks one model that he controls that is engaged, and has yet to fight this turn, and that combat is resolved. Then the other player picks a model that he controls that is in combat and resolves it, and this process continues until all combats have been resolved. Each model will only fight one round of combat under normal circumstances.

COMBAT PROCESS

1. The player with Priority picks one model that he controls that is engaged.
2. Players secretly draw counters equal to the value of the Combat Pool of the models that they control that are involved in the combat, choosing between Attack and Defence Counters.
3. Each player then reveals his Combat Pool, placing it in front of him.
4. Initiative is determined. Each player rolls a d6 (2d6 if he chooses to Enhance, discarding one die – see rules for Enhancing below) for each model that he controls in the combat, adding the relevant model's Initiative Characteristic and any other modifiers. The result is the model's Initiative score for this combat, and determines the order in which models have the opportunity to declare an attack. In the case of a draw, the models involved roll off to see who goes first, adding no modifiers and with no further opportunity for Enhancing. If this is drawn, they roll again, and so on.
5. The model with the highest Initiative has the option to make one or more attacks (see below). However, that model may instead elect to pass and not make an attack.
6. Once this has been resolved the model with the next highest Initiative score has the opportunity to declare an attack, and so on, returning to the model with the highest Initiative.
7. Once all models have emptied their Combat Pool, or each model has passed once in succession, the combat is over.

Minowa Castle, 1564, by Johnny Shumate
© Osprey Publishing Ltd. Taken from Weapon 5: *Katana: The Samurai Sword.*

MAKING AN ATTACK

1. Nominate the model to make the attack (the Attacker) and the target of the attack (the Defender).
2. Remove an Attack Counter from the Attacker's Combat Pool.
3. The Defender may choose to Enhance his Defence Roll (see below for details). If he chooses to do so, remove one Defence Counter from his Combat Pool.
4. The Attacker may now choose to Enhance his Attack Roll (see below for details). If he chooses to do so, remove one additional Attack Counter from his Combat Pool.
5. The Attacker may choose to declare a Special Attack (see below).
6. The Attacker rolls 2d6 (3d6 if he chooses to Enhance, discarding one die – see rules for Enhancing below) and adds his Fight Characteristic and any special modifiers. This is the Attack Roll.
7. The Defender rolls 1d6 (2d6 if he chose to Enhance, keeping both dice – see rules for Enhancing below) and adds his Fight Characteristic, modifiers for armour and any special modifiers. This is the Defence Roll.
8. Subtract the Defence Roll from the Attack Roll – this is the Wound Score. If the Wound Score is 1 or more, then a wound may have been caused. Refer to the Wound Table (page 19). If the Wound Score is 0 or negative, the attack has failed.

Modifiers to Defence Roll	
Target has light armour	+1
Target has medium armour	+2
Target has heavy armour	+3
Target is engaged by 3 or more enemy models	-1

ENHANCING ROLLS

At certain points in the Combat Phase, a model may Enhance its roll by removing a counter from its Combat Pool. Only one Enhancement may ever be applied to a single roll. The opportunities for Enhancing and the rules governing them are as follows:

- Enhancing Initiative: Before the dice are rolled to determine Initiative, any model can discard an Attack Counter from his Combat Pool to roll an additional die and then choose which one to keep.
- Enhance Defence Roll: The Defender may choose to Enhance his Defence Roll if he has at least one Defence Counter in his Combat Pool. Remove this Defence Counter, and the player may roll an additional d6 as part of the Defence Roll.
- Enhance Attack Roll: The Attacker may choose to Enhance his Attack Roll if he has at least one Attack Counter in his Combat Pool. Remove this Attack Counter, and the player may roll an additional d6 as part of the Attack Roll, and then choose which two dice are retained, discarding the third.

Summary: Enhancing is different for each situation
When you Enhance an Initiative Roll, you roll 2 dice and discard 1.
When you Enhance an Attack Roll, you roll 3 dice and discard 1.
When you Enhance a Defence Roll, you roll 2 dice and keep both.

MULTIPLE COMBATS

A model may never make more attacks than its Combat Pool Characteristic. As has been mentioned, in a combat where multiple models are fighting on the same side, their Combat Pools are combined. So, in order to ensure that no model expends too many Counters, it is important to keep track of which models have done what.

This is best done by placing counters next to models as they expend them. Additionally, a model may expend a Defence Counter to Enhance the Defence Roll of another model, but may only ever expend Attack Counters on its own attacks.

HAND-TO-HAND WEAPONS

Weapon	Initiative Modifier	Attack Roll Modifier	Special
Katana (sword)			
Wakizashi (short sword)	-1		
Nodachi (two-handed sword)	-1	+1	
Tanto (dagger)	-1	-1	
Naginata (halberd)	+1	+1	
Yari (spear)	+2		+1 Attack Roll Modifier if mounted and making a ride-by attack.
Nagae-yari (pike)	+3/-2		This weapon provides a +3 Initiative bonus in the first round of combat. However, if this same combat continues for another turn, the wielder suffers a -2 Initiative penalty for each subsequent turn.
Jo (short staff)	+1		
Bo (quarterstaff)			
Tetsubo (long club)	-1	+1	
Kasurigama (sickle and chain)	+1/-		This weapon provides a +1 Initiative bonus in the first round of combat and +1 to any Subdue attempt.
Weaponless	-1	-1	This represents fighting without a weapon, using punches, kicks and grappling techniques. Such attacks suffer an additional -1 penalty when directed against models equipped with heavy armour.
Improvised weapon	-1		

WHICH WEAPON?

Many models are equipped with multiple weapons in *Ronin*. One of these will be the model's primary weapon, which will usually be the one that the actual figure is using. However, at the start of each combat, the player controlling the model may declare that it is using a different weapon. A model may switch weapons during a combat (for example, if it is disarmed), but this will cost an Attack Counter, and the switch happens instead of the model in question making an attack.

Okehazama, 1560, by Angus McBride
© Osprey Publishing Ltd. Taken from Elite 23: *The Samurai*.

SPECIAL ATTACKS

There are two types of special attacks that can be made – Disarm and Subdue. These attacks are declared after counters have been allocated but before Initiative is rolled.

When making a Disarm attack, a model attempts to destroy or otherwise make unusable its opponent's weapon. No special rules apply, and if at least a Grievous wound is caused by the attack, it is successful. No wound is actually caused, but the defending model loses the use of the weapon it was fighting with and must use another. If it is not equipped with another weapon, it is considered weaponless. If only a Stunned or Light wound is caused, or if the attack is not successful, then there is no effect.

A Subdue attack is an attempt to capture an opponent without causing it harm. As with Disarm, if at least a Grievous wound is caused by the attack, it is successful. No wound is actually caused, but the defending model cannot take any action, fight in combat, move etc. while it remains in contact with any enemy model. If more than one model is engaging the defending model when the Subdue special attack is attempted, these can contribute to the Subdue attempt by removing one additional Attack Counter for each model in addition to the first. Each additional Attack Counter adds +1 to the Attack Roll. Unlike a Disarm attack, any Light wound or Stunned result still count as normal, though the Subdue will not have worked.

WOUNDS

There are four types of wounds that models can suffer. These are represented by placing the relevant marker next to the model. A model may accrue any number of Stunned markers, but will only ever have one Light or Grievous wound, and never both at the same time, as is explained further below. Stunned markers are periodically removed as part of the game, but Light and Grievous wound markers remain in place for the rest of the game.

WOUND DESCRIPTIONS

- Stunned: A minor blow that disorientates the model and stops it from acting at full capacity for a short period of time. A model may accumulate any number of Stunned results, but these do not stack with each other, so the effects are only applied once. However, because Stunned counters are removed randomly, a model may remain Stunned for more than one turn.
- Light wounds: These wounds only slightly affect a model's capacity to act, but are potentially serious.
- Grievous wound: This type of wound is very serious and may well prove fatal in time.
- Critical wound: These are fatal wounds. Remove the model and indicate its place on the board with a Slain marker, as the body of the fallen warrior may yet play a part in the game.

WOUND TABLE

Use the table below to determine whether or not a wound has been caused.

Wound Score	Result	Effect
1	Stunned	-1 to Initiative
2–3	Light wound	-1 to Initiative, -1 to Fight
4–5	Grievous wound	-2 to Initiative, -1 to Fight, -1 to Combat Pool, -1 to Shoot
6	Critical wound	This model has been killed

- If a model with a Light wound suffers another Light wound, it will immediately become a Grievous wound.
- If a model with a Grievous wound suffers any sort of wound, it will immediately become a Critical wound.
- Wounds come into effect immediately, so if a model that is in combat and has yet to attack suffers a Grievous wound, its statistics (including Combat Pool) immediately drop by the indicated amount. It is up to the controlling player to decide how to reduce a model's Combat Pool when this occurs. If it has no counters left in its Combat Pool, then this effect is ignored.

COMBAT EXAMPLE

In this example, a Samurai armed with a naginata (controlled by Player A) is fighting 2 Ashigaru, one armed with a yari and one with a katana (controlled by Player B).

The first step is to determine the Combat Pools for each side. The Samurai has a Combat Pool Characteristic of 3 and, deciding to hedge his bets, Player A secretly chooses two black counters (for Attack) and one white counter (for Defence). Player B has a Combat Pool of 4 (as both Ashigaru have a Combat Pool Characteristic of 2), and he chooses 2 counters for Attack and 2 for Defence.

The next step is to determine Initiative. Player A rolls one d6 whilst Player B rolls two d6, being careful to indicate which die relates to which of his two models. The Samurai scores a 3 which, combined with his Initiative Characteristic of 3 and a +1 bonus for his naginata, gives a score of 7. The Ashigaru with the yari rolled a 4, which also gives him a total of 7, while the Ashigaru with the katana rolls a 3, giving him a total of 5. The Samurai and the Ashigaru with the yari do a straight roll off with no modifiers, with the Samurai rolling a 5 and the Ashigaru a 2. So the Samurai will have the first attack opportunity, the Ashigaru with the yari the second, and the Ashigaru with the katana will go last.

The Samurai elects to attack the Ashigaru with the yari. He removes a black counter from his Combat Pool. The Ashigaru decides to Enhance his Defence Roll, so he removes a white counter from his Combat Pool. The Samurai player elects to not Enhance his Attack Roll, and so the dice are now rolled.

The Samurai rolls a 4 and a 5. As he has chosen the Naginatatjutsu Attribute, he could choose to re-roll one of these dice, but he is quite happy with his score of 9. Added to his Fight Characteristic of 3 and a +1 modifier for his Naginata, this gives him an Attack Roll of 13. The Ashigaru player rolls a 4 and a 1, giving him a score of 5. He adds +2 to this for his medium armour and another 2 for his Fight Characteristic, giving him a Defence Roll of 9.

The Samurai has caused a wound as the Attack Roll is greater than the Defence Roll. Referring to the Wound Table shows that a difference of 4 causes a Grievous wound. The Ashigaru with the yari will suffer -2 to Initiative and -1 to his Fight for the rest of the game. His Combat Pool is also reduced by 1, and since this takes effect immediately, Player B must discard one counter from his Combat Pool. He chooses to discard a white counter, leaving two black (attack) counters in his Combat Pool.

This completes the Samurai's attack. The model with the next highest initiative is the Ashigaru with the yari. However, he has already expended a Defence Counter in his futile attempt to parry the Samurai's attack, and because of the Grievous wound that he suffered, his Combat Pool has decreased by 1. So this model cannot make any further attacks.

Therefore, it falls to the last Ashigaru, armed with a katana, to make an attack. He chooses to do so, and removes one black counter. The Samurai player, sensing the desperation of his opponent, elects to Enhance his Defence Roll, and so removes his only white counter. The Ashigaru player now elects to Enhance his Attack Roll, and so removes his last black counter.

The dice are now rolled. The Ashigaru rolls three dice because it is a Enhanceed Attack. He gets a 3, 4 and 6, and discards the 3. Added to his Fight Characteristic of 2, this gives him an attack roll of 12.

The Samurai player rolls 2 dice, getting a 2 and a 3. This time, he elects to use his Naginatatjutsu Attribute and re-rolls the 2, getting a 3. Hardly much better, but when adding this total of 6 to his Fight Characteristic of 3 as well as +3 for his heavy armour, it gives him a score of 12. As the scores are the same, no wound is caused.

The opportunity to make another attack now returns to the Samurai. As he has a single black counter remaining, he declares an attack on the grievously wounded Ashigaru. Player B has no counters left in his Combat Pool, so it is down to the dice rolls. The Samurai rolls a 2 and a 4. He elects to use his Naginatatjutsu Attribute to re-roll the 2, but this time gets a 1, which he must keep. Added to his Fight of 3 and adding +1 for the naginata, this gives him an Attack Roll of 9. The hapless Ashigaru rolls a 4 which, added to his Fight of 2 and his medium armour gives him an 8. However, his Grievous wound means that his Fight Characteristic is at -1, reducing his Defence Roll to just 7. A Light wound has been caused which, combined with the Grievous wound, means that the Ashigaru with the yari has suffered a Critical wound. The model is removed and a Slain marker is put in its place.

Things are looking grim for the remaining Ashigaru, while the Samurai is anticipating the opportunity of collecting two heads for his daimyo...

ACTION PHASE

During this phase, models that are not engaged may undertake one of the following actions:

- Use a missile weapon
- Reload a teppo
- Loot a body or collect a head
- Pick up an object
- Mount or dismount
- Rest

Starting with the player with Priority, each player selects an eligible model and performs one of these actions until no eligible models remain.

USE A MISSILE WEAPON

See the rules in the Move Phase for using missile weapons.

RELOAD A TEPPO

The matchlock firearm known as the teppo is slow to reload once it has been fired. If a model armed with a teppo did not move, did not shoot, is not Stunned and did not fight in hand-to-hand combat this turn, it may reload. Remove the counter signifying that the teppo has been fired to denote that it is available to be fired again from the beginning of the next turn. Note that teppos are considered to begin the game loaded and ready to be fired.

LOOT A BODY OR COLLECT A HEAD

Any model that is not Stunned and/or not engaged, and is also in base-to-base contact with a Slain marker, may loot that body or collect its head during this phase.

PICK UP AN OBJECT

Any model that is not Stunned and/or not engaged may pick up an object during this phase. This will generally be a scenario requirement. There are two types of objects. Light objects can be picked up and carried by a single model without any hindrance. Examples include weapons, banners, small boxes, and so on. Heavy objects can be picked up by a single model, but that model will be Encumbered and will move only at half pace. Alternatively, two models that are both in base-to-base contact with a heavy object may carry it without penalty. In this case, both models are activated simultaneously. Examples of heavy objects include bodies and large chests. A model that is carrying an object is assumed to drop it if engaged by the enemy. However, it can choose not to drop it, in which case it suffers a -1 penalty to all Initiative, Attack and Defence Rolls

MOUNT OR DISMOUNT

Any model that is not Stunned and/or not engaged may mount or dismount during this phase. Note that a model may only mount if it is adjacent to a horse and if it could normally be allowed to be fielded as mounted. See Special Rules for more information on mounted models.

REST

A model may rest during this phase, in which case it gains a +1 modifier when rolling to remove Stunned counters in the End Phase.

END PHASE

REMOVE STUNNED COUNTERS

Roll a d6 for each model that has one or more Stunned counters and apply the result shown in the table below. Apply a -1 modifier to this roll if the model is engaged in combat, and a +1 modifier if the model rested in the Action Phase.

1–2	No effect.
3–5	Remove one Stunned Counter
6	Remove up to two Stunned Counters

VICTORY CONDITIONS

Check to see if the Victory Conditions of the scenario have been met.

SPECIAL RULES

BANNERS

Large banners were common in many armies of the era, and as in other cultures were used as rallying points and to inspire troops. Certain factions in *Ronin* may field banners as part of their Buntai, as indicated in the Faction rules. The following rules apply to models that are carrying banners:

- The model may not voluntarily engage in combat.
- If engaged in combat by the enemy, the model suffers a -1 penalty to all Initiative, Attack and Defence Rolls. The model may only use a katana (or equivalent) in combat.
- If the model carrying the banner is killed, the banner is left and may be picked up by any model in the Action Phase.
- Banners are worth Victory Points if captured by the enemy, as detailed under Scenarios.
- While the banner is in the possession of a living model, the Buntai may re-roll failed Morale Tests.

MOUNTED MODELS

Models that are mounted on a horse have special rules for combat and movement.

Mounted models may move up to 12" in the Move Phase and still engage in combat. A mounted model may make a Gallop move up to 18" as long as it does not move within 1" of an enemy model. Mounted models may not enter difficult terrain or buildings.

A mounted model may also choose to make a ride-by attack (see below).

FIGHTING WHEN MOUNTED

Fighting while mounted incurs a -2 penalty to the Attack Roll. Using a yumi while mounted incurs a -2 penalty to the Shooting Attack Roll. A teppo may not be used while mounted. Models with the Bajutsu Attribute will ignore these penalties.

A foot model that is in combat with a mounted model may choose to attack either the mount or its rider. In mounted-versus-mounted combat, the riders must attack each other. When attacking a mount, it is considered to have a Fight Characteristic of 1 and no armour but always has Enhanced Defence Rolls. If a mount suffers a Grievous wound (or worse) then its rider is immediately thrown (see below).

SHOOTING AT MOUNTED MODELS

There are two ways to shoot at a mounted model. The shooter can attempt to target either the rider or the mount, which will incur an additional -1 penalty to the Shooting Attack Roll. Otherwise, before making the Shooting Attack Roll, roll a d6. On a result of 1–4 the target of the attack is the mount, and on a 5–6 it is the rider. Mounts are considered to have light armour against shooting attacks, which is automatically negated if shot at by a teppo.

RIDE-BY ATTACK

A ride-by attack is a special type of attack that can only be made by mounted models. Unlike other movement, this happens in the Combat Phase. To be eligible to make a ride-by attack, the model must not already be engaged and must not have moved this turn. The model is activated in the Combat Phase (ignoring the normal rule of only activating models that are in combat). The model is then moved up to 9" into base-to-base contact with one or more enemy models. A combat is fought as usual, except that all models must halve their Combat Pool (rounding up, with a minimum of one). The rider has an Initiative bonus of +1 in this combat. As soon as the combat is resolved, the mounted model may, if able, immediately move up to 9" (not passing within 1" of an enemy model).

THROWN RIDERS

When a rider is thrown, replace the mounted model with a foot model and give this model a Stunned counter. The mount leaves play and cannot be used again.

WARHORSES

Some horses are particularly suited to combat – Samurai often rode ungelded stallions into battle to capitalise on the animal's natural aggression. Warhorses have a Fight Characteristic of 1, a single Attack Counter and an Initiative of 1, and fight in combat like all other models. If the combat is between two mounted models, the warhorse must attack the other mount.

ATTRIBUTES

Some models have exceptional skills and abilities, referred to as Attributes, that allow them to do things that other models cannot. These are generally only available to high-ranked models. There are two types of Attributes – Abilities and Bujutsu (Japanese for 'martial art'). There are many sub-types of Bujutsu, as explained below, and each of these counts as an Attribute in its own right.

ABILITIES

Acrobatic	This model is extremely agile and not affected by Difficult terrain, and also counts Impassable terrain as Difficult terrain. Also, this model may not be attacked if it chooses to Withdraw. Finally, this model can move through friendly models so long as there is room for the model's base wherever it completes its movement.
Commander	If a Buntai has at least one model with this ability, it gets a -1 modifier on any Morale check.
Fast	This model gains +1 to all Initiative Rolls and automatically wins any Initiative draws.
Fearless	This model ignores the results of any Morale Test.
Inexorable	A model with Inexorable may move short distances and attack different models during a single Combat Phase. If a model with this ability kills all of the models that it is fighting in the Combat Phase (in other words, inflicts Critical wounds on them all) it may immediately move up to 2" into base-to-base contact with another enemy model. If this model still has at least one Attack Counter in its Combat pool, it may use this move to engage another enemy model. This may result in a number of situations: • If the enemy model is not currently engaged and has not yet been activated this turn, then it must draw counters equal to its Combat Pool and it fights a combat. The attacking model, however, is limited to the Attack Counters that remained from the previous combat that it fought. • If the enemy model is not currently engaged but has already been activated this turn, then it is allocated a single Defence Counter and the two models fight a combat. The attacking model is still limited to the Attack Counters that remained from the previous combat that it fought. • If the model has no option other than to engage more than one enemy model when using this ability (i.e. moves into base-to-base contact with several models) then it must fight all of them using the rules above.
Intuition	This model gains one free Defence Counter each turn.
Powerful	This model gains +1 to all Attack Rolls.
Tough	This model is particularly hardy and ignores the effects of Light wounds. However, the model still counts as having a Light wound, so if it suffers an additional Light wound it will have a Grievous wound, and so on. Additionally, if this model suffers a Critical wound it is not removed until the end of the current Combat Phase, and so may have the opportunity to make a final attack.
Yojimbo	Yojimbo is Japanese for 'bodyguard'. Once per game, at the beginning of the turn, you may choose to physically swap this model with the Leader of its Buntai as long as the two models are within 3" of each other. Additionally, once per turn, if the highest ranking model in the Buntai is the target of a shooting attack, that attack may be directed at the model with Yojimbo instead if it is within 3".

BUJUTSU

Bujutsu literally means 'martial art'. The study and perfection of martial skills is common in all cultures, but the Japanese are rightly famous for taking this to a new level.

In *Ronin* there are two types of Bujutsu – Weapons Bujutsu and Advanced Bujutsu.

Hachimanbara, 1561, by Wayne Reynolds
© Osprey Publishing Ltd. Taken from Campaign 130: *Kawanakajima 1553–64.*

WEAPONS BUJUTSU

Each type of Bujutsu is linked to a particular weapon type, giving that model an advantage when wielding that weapon. When using that weapon, the model is permitted to re-roll one Attack or Defence Roll die each time time it makes an Attack or Defence Roll (or Shooting Attack Roll if the Bujutsu relates to a missile weapon). If this ability is used in conjunction with a Enhanceed Attack Roll, the re-roll must be done AFTER the additional die is discarded.

Bujutsu	Weapon	Special
Kenjutsu	Katana/wakizashi/nodachi	
Naginatatjutsu	Naginata	
Sojutsu	Yari	
Jojutsu	Jo	
Bojutsu	Bo	
Tetsubojutsu	Tetsubo	
Kasurigamajustsu	Kasurigama	+1 to Subdue and Disarm special attacks
Jujutsu	Weaponless	+1 to Subdue special attacks
Kyujutsu	Yumi	
Hojutsu	Teppo	

ADVANCED BUJUTSU

Bujutsu	Effect
Niten (two swords)	This art requires the model to already have the Kenjutsu proficiency. The model may fight with a katana in one hand and wakizashi in the other, which increases the model's Combat Pool by +1.
Yadome-jutsu (arrow stopping)	This art requires the model to already be proficient in any of the Weapons Bujustu. All attacks from yumi against this model suffer an additional -2 penalty to the Attack Roll on top of any other modifiers.
Bajutsu (horse riding)	This art allows the model to fight while mounted without any penalty.
Senjo-jutsu (tactics)	This art allows the player to either re-roll the Priority die roll or force his opponent to re-roll his Priority die roll.

FACTIONS

The following list of factions allows players to build a Buntai to play *Ronin*. Buntai means roughly 'squad' or 'team' in Japanese, and is used in these rules for what are loose collections of warriors.

Each Faction listing has detailed rules and information about that particular faction. 100 points is enough for a small game of *Ronin* playable in about an hour, and for most factions this will require fewer than 10 models.

Each Faction listing has the following sections:

BACKGROUND
A brief background for the faction.

COMPOSITION
This section provides rules for how many models of each type can be fielded, and also outlines limits on certain weapons, particularly missile weapons. Where the rules refer to a percentage limit on a particular weapon, always round down. For example, no more than 25% of the Models in a Bushi Buntai may be armed with teppos. So if you have 8 models, 2 may be armed with teppos. But if you have 10 models, the teppo limit is still 2.

SPECIAL RULES

This section details any special rules that apply to the faction with regards to weapons, Victory Points or banners.

MORALE

This lists the Morale Rating of the faction and any special rules relating to Morale.

SWORDS-FOR-HIRE

A list of the Swords-for-Hire available to this faction. No more than 25% of the number of Models in your Buntai may be Swords-for-Hire.

MODEL LIST

This is the complete list of models belonging to the faction and the options available to them. It is very important that the models that you field match as exactly as possible the description of the model. So if you select a Samurai with a yumi in your Buntai, then you must have a Samurai figure with a yumi to put on the tabletop!

Each Buntai must have a Leader, which will always be the highest ranked model. If more than one model of the same rank is fielded, the player decides which is to be the Leader.

BUSHI

'Having been born into the house of a warrior, one's intentions should be to grasp the long and the short swords and to die.' – Kato Kiyomasa (1562–1611)

BACKGROUND

Bushi are the professional soldiers of this period, the Ashigaru and the Samurai. These would serve a single lord, or daimyo, who provided for their equipment and upkeep.

Ashigaru (literally 'light foot') were the common infantry, equipped with mass-produced arms and armour by their daimyo and trained to fight en masse with yari or yumi. Despite their lowly status, during this period of Japanese history Ashigaru could still hope to rise through the ranks, as the great general Toyotomi Hideyoshi did. Units of Ashigaru were commanded by Gashira or Go-gashira – captains and lieutenants. Ashigaru could be distinguished by the distinctive conical helmets (called jingasa), which often bore the mon (a type of family crest) of their daimyo.

Samurai formed the elite warrior caste and trained in the use of multiple weapons. Although the paired swords and particularly the katana were closely associated with the Samurai, he was just as likely to fight with a spear or the deadly polearm known as the naginata. Samurai also trained in the use of the yumi and even the teppo. Samurai armour was more substantial and much more ornate than Ashigaru armour, and they would often wear a sashimono, a flag attached to the back plate of their armour. Samurai sought single combat with worthy opponents, rather than fighting en masse. Even the Samurai had ranks, with the elite being the hatamoto ('horse guards') who were the bodyguards of the daimyo.

Bushi are the default faction for *Ronin*, and historically fought against all of the other factions as well as each other! This is a strong faction and has access to the best arms and armour and a range of skills and abilities.

Opposite:
Chikumagawa Ford, 1561, by Wayne Reynolds
© Osprey Publishing Ltd. Taken from Campaign 130: *Kawanakajima 1553–64.*

COMPOSITION

- There must be at least two Rank 1 and/or Rank 2 models for each Rank 3 or higher model; OR each model in the Buntai must be Rank 3 or higher.
- There must be at least three Rank 1 models for each Rank 2 model (if any Rank 1 or 2 models are selected).
- For each Rank 4 model, there must be at least one Rank 3 model.
- There may only be one Rank 5 model.
- No more than 25% of the models may be armed with a teppo, and no more than 50% may have a missile weapon.

SPECIAL RULES

Models in this Faction score Victory Points in the following manner, in addition to any scenario-specific conditions:

- Each friendly model killed by an enemy model of a lower rank: -1
- Each head of an enemy model that was collected by a Samurai still alive at the end of the game: +1

Additionally, if the game is lost but the Bushi Leader is still alive at the end of the game, he may commit seppuku to score an additional 2 Victory Points. This may never result in the Bushi winning the game (even if the seppuku gives them the most points), but may create a draw.

One Ashigaru or Ashigaru-gashira may carry a banner. A banner bearer may only use a katana, so an Ashigaru given a banner costs -3 points and loses the option of carrying a yari, nagae-yari, yumi or teppo. An Ashigaru-gashira may take a banner for no cost, but may not be given additional equipment. This banner is called a nobori and will usually display the daimyo's personal mon and other heraldic symbols.

Due to the relatively high points cost of Bushi models, a player may find himself quite a few points short of an agreed points total when selecting his Buntai. He may, however, purchase up to three Fearsome Kiai options for 5 points each. Each Fearsome Kiai expended allows the Bushi player to automatically win Priority, and must be declared before any dice are rolled in the Priority Phase. If two players attempt to use Fearsome Kiai in the same turn, then roll as usual.

MORALE

The Morale Rating of Bushi is 9.

SWORDS-FOR-HIRE

Bushi may hire Ronin, Warrior Monks (limit of one) or Ninja (limit of one). If a Ninja is hired, the Bushi will suffer a -1 Victory Point penalty.

MODEL LIST

ASHIGARU

Type	Rank	CP	Initiative	Fight	Shoot	Armour	Points
Ashigaru	1	2	2	2	1	Medium	18
Weapons	Katana and either yari, nagae-yari, yumi or teppo						
Attributes	None						
Options	• May be fielded with no armour for -4 points						

ASHIGARU-GASHIRA

Type	Rank	CP	Initiative	Fight	Shoot	Armour	Points
Ashigaru	2	2	2	3	1	Medium	18
Weapons	Katana						
Attributes	Commander						
Options	• May have one of yari, nagae-yari, teppo or yumi for +3 points • May be fielded with no armour for -4 points						

SAMURAI

Type	Rank	CP	Initiative	Fight	Shoot	Armour	Points
Samurai	3	3	3	3	2	Heavy	24
Weapons	Katana and wakizashi						
Attributes	Commander and may choose one additional Attribute for +3 points						
Options	• May have one of naginata, nodachi, yari, tetsubo, teppo or yumi for +3 points • May be fielded with no armour for -6 points.						

HATAMOTO

Type	Rank	CP	Initiative	Fight	Shoot	Armour	Points
Samurai	4	4	4	4	2	Heavy	29
Weapons	Katana and wakizashi						
Attributes	Commander and may choose up to two additional Attributes for +3 points each						
Options	• May have one of naginata, nodachi, yari, tetsubo, teppo or yumi for +3 points • May be mounted on a horse for +10 points or a warhorse for +15 points • May be fielded with no armour for -6 points						

BUSHOU

Type	Rank	CP	Initiative	Fight	Shoot	Armour	Points
Samurai	5	5	4	5	3	Heavy	34
Weapons	Katana and wakizashi						
Attributes	Commander and may choose up to three additional Attributes for +3 points each						
Options	• May have one of naginata, nodachi, yari, tetsubo, teppo or yumi for +3 points • May be mounted on a horse for +10 points or a warhorse for +15 points • May be fielded with no armour for -6 points						

IKKO-IKKI

'Renounce this defiled world and attain the Pure Land' – Ikko-Ikki slogan, 16th century

BACKGROUND

The Ikko-Ikki, or 'Single-minded League', was the largest and most successful of a curious group of Japanese religious and social movements. Adherents of the Jodo-Shinshu Buddhist sect, the Ikko-Ikki rebelled

against local daimyos and eventually gained control of 3 entire provinces. Ikko-Ikki armies were large and diverse, comprising a mixture of peasants, foot soldiers (known as Monto), warrior monks and even Samurai. Many would have ad hoc armour and weapons, but many would also be virtually indistinguishable from their Bushi equivalents.

The Ikko-Ikki fought many battles against the Bushi and Sohei. The great Samurai warlords Tokugawa Ieyasu and Oda Nobunaga eventually destroyed them as a major force in Japan. The Ikko-Ikki did not take part in the Imjin War, so never faced the Koreans or Chinese in battle.

The Ikko-Ikki is a strong faction quite capable of taking on the Bushi.

COMPOSITION
- There must be more Rank 0 and Rank 1 models than Rank 2 or higher.
- There must be at least 3 Rank 1 models for each Rank 2 model.
- There may only be one Rank 4 model.
- No more than 25% of the models may be armed with a teppo, and no more than 50% may have a missile weapon.

SPECIAL RULES
Ikko-Ikki often carried large banners into battle with Buddhist slogans on them. Any Monto or Monto-gashira may carry a banner for no cost, and may not be given any additional equipment.

MORALE
The Morale Rating of Ikko-Ikki is 8, or 9 if the Buntai has a banner.

SWORDS-FOR-HIRE
Ikko-Ikki may hire Ronin or Ninja (limit of one).

MODEL LIST

PEASANT

Type	Rank	CP	Initiative	Fight	Shoot	Armour	Points
Peasant	0	1	1	1	0	None	4
Weapons	Improvised weapon						
Attributes	None						
Options	• May have yari for +4 points						

MONTO

Type	Rank	CP	Initiative	Fight	Shoot	Armour	Points
Monto	1	2	2	2	1	Light	13
Weapons	Katana						
Attributes	None						
Options	• May have one of yari, nagae-yari, teppo or yumi for +3 points • May be fielded with no armour for -2 points						

MONTO-GASHIRA

Type	Rank	CP	Initiative	Fight	Shoot	Armour	Points
Samurai	2	2	2	3	1	Medium	18
Weapons	Katana						
Attributes	Commander						
Options	• May have one of yari, nagae-yari, teppo or yumi for +3 points • May be fielded with no armour for -4 points						

SAMURAI

Type	Rank	CP	Initiative	Fight	Shoot	Armour	Points
Samurai	3	3	3	3	2	Heavy	24
Weapons	Katana and wakizashi						
Attributes	Commander and may choose one additional Attribute for +3 points						
Options	• May have one of naginata, nodachi, yari, tetsubo, teppo or yumi for +3 points • May be fielded with no armour for -6 points						

SOHEI

Type	Rank	CP	Initiative	Fight	Shoot	Armour	Points
Sohei	3	3	3	3	2	Medium	26
Weapons	Katana and one of naginata, tetsubo, yumi or teppo						
Attributes	Fearless and may choose one additional Attribute for +3 points						
Options	• May be fielded with no armour for -4 points						

HANSHOU

Type	Rank	CP	Initiative	Fight	Shoot	Armour	Points
Samurai	4	4	4	4	2	Heavy	29
Weapons	Katana and wakizashi						
Attributes	Commander and may choose up to two additional Attributes for +3 points each						
Options	• May have one of naginata, nodachi, yari, tetsubo, teppo or yumi for +3 points • May be mounted on a horse for +10 points or a warhorse for +15 points • May be fielded with no armour for -6 points						

SOHEI

'Thereupon a monk kicked over the shield in front of him and sprang forward, whirling his naginata like a water wheel.' – Account of the 14th-century attack of the Mount Hei monastery on Kyoto from the *Taiheiki*

Sohei defend Kyoto against the Ikko-Ikki, by
Wayne Reynolds © Osprey Publishing Ltd.
Taken from Warrior 70: *Japanese Warrior Monks
AD 949–1603.*

BACKGROUND

Sects of Buddhist warrior monks known as Sohei could be found in
temples across Japan during this period. The Sohei are strongly associated
with the Ikko-Ikki, but are entirely separate and predate that particular
movement by many centuries. Sohei monasteries could be relatively small
affairs in remote areas or the equivalent of small towns with thousands
of residents. While not fundamentally aggressive, the Sohei had no
hesitation in taking up arms if they or their interests were threatened. As
such, they fought in many campaigns during the Sengoku Jidai with and
against the Samurai and Ikko-Ikki, though they did not take part in the
invasion of Korea.

Sohei wore priest-like robes over their armour, and often had shaved
heads or wore a cowl. Sohei were famed for their martial skill, particularly
with the naginata, but they were proficient in many other weapons,
including the teppo and yumi. Though not diverse, the Sohei form a solid
faction that can hold its own against the other factions.

COMPOSITION

* There may only be one Rank 5 model.
* No more than 25% of the models may be armed with a teppo, and no
  more than 50% may have a missile weapon.

SPECIAL RULES

No special rules apply to the Sohei.

MORALE

Most Sohei are Fearless and so never check Morale. Temple Attendants test on a Morale of 7.

SWORDS-FOR-HIRE

Sohei may not use Swords-for-Hire.

MODEL LIST

TEMPLE ATTENDANT

Type	Rank	CP	Initiative	Fight	Shoot	Armour	Points
Sohei	1	1	1	1	0	None	8
Weapons	Yari						
Attributes	Fearless when within 3" of any model of Rank 2 or higher						
Options	• None						

INITIATE

Type	Rank	CP	Initiative	Fight	Shoot	Armour	Points
Sohei	2	2	2	3	1	Medium	19
Weapons	Katana and one of naginata, tetsubo, yumi or teppo						
Attributes	Fearless						
Options	• May be fielded with no armour for -4 points						

SOHEI

Type	Rank	CP	Initiative	Fight	Shoot	Armour	Points
Sohei	3	3	3	3	2	Medium	26
Weapons	Katana and one of naginata, tetsubo or yumi						
Attributes	Fearless and may choose one additional Attribute for +3 points						
Options	• May be fielded with no armour for -4 points						

SENIOR SOHEI

Type	Rank	CP	Initiative	Fight	Shoot	Armour	Points
Sohei	4	4	4	4	2	Medium	31
Weapons	Katana and one of naginata, tetsubo or yumi						
Attributes	Fearless and may choose up to two additional Attributes for +3 points each						
Options	• May be fielded with no armour for -4 points						

GRANDMASTER

Type	Rank	CP	Initiative	Fight	Shoot	Armour	Points
Sohei	5	5	4	5	3	Medium	36
Weapons	Katana and one of naginata, tetsubo or yumi						
Attributes	Fearless and may choose up to three additional Attributes for +3 points each						
Options	• May be fielded with no armour for -4 points						

KORYU

'From one thing, know ten thousand things.' – Miyamoto Musashi (1584–1645), *Go Rin No Sho*

BACKGROUND

Koryu means roughly 'traditional school' and represents the martial arts schools of medieval Japan. There were hundreds of such schools specialising in different weapons and fighting techniques, and many have survived to this day. Some Koryu would be relatively small affairs, with just a handful of students studying under a single master in a secluded place, while others would be large institutions in major population centres. Most Koryu would specialise in one particular weapon or technique, but most would also provide less intense training in others. A good example of an actual Koryu is Shinto Muso-ryu jojutsu, founded in the early 17th century by Muso Gonnosuke Katsuyoshi. The principal weapon of this art is the jo, with 6 series of kata ('forms of practice') totalling more than 50 techniques. However, Shinto Muso-ryu practioners also trained with a number of other weapons, including the katana, wakizashi, kasurigama and walking stick. Competition between schools could often be fierce, leading to many duels both formal and spontaneous.

This is a specialist faction, and its lack of armour means that it will be at a disadvantage against factions such as Bushi.

COMPOSITION

- There may only be one Rank 5 model.

SPECIAL RULES

Most Koryu specialise in one type of weapon, with limited training in others. When selecting a Koryu Buntai, one melee weapon must be chosen as the primary weapon of the Koryu from the list below, and up to two others may be chosen as secondary weapons. At least half the models in the Buntai must be armed with the Koryu's primary weapon. Although Koryu existed that specialised in missile weapons, this can be unbalancing in game terms so that option has not been included here. However, if you feel differently you are welcome to try it.

Weapon	Points cost per model
Katana	+0
Wakizashi	+0
Nodachi	+3
Naginata	+3
Yari	+3
Jo	+0
Bo	+0
Tetsubo	+3
Kasurigama	+0
Weaponless	+0

The profile for each model that is eligible to have an Attribute has already been assigned the Bujutsu for the Koryu's primary weapon, and the points cost of this Bujutsu is already included in the model's cost. Other Attributes may be chosen as normal.

Each model that fights in combat with its Koryu's primary weapon earns the Buntai an additional 1 Victory Point at the end of the game if it survives.

MORALE

The Morale Rating of Koryu is 9 as long as the Sensei is still on the table (and alive). Otherwise, it drops to 7.

SWORDS-FOR-HIRE

Koryu may hire a Shugyosha.

MODEL LIST

NOVICE

Type	Rank	CP	Initiative	Fight	Shoot	Armour	Points
Koryu	1	1	1	2	0	None	7
Weapons	Special						
Attributes	None						
Options	• None						

INITIATE

Type	Rank	CP	Initiative	Fight	Shoot	Armour	Points
Koryu	2	2	2	2	1	None	14
Weapons	Special						
Attributes	Bujutsu for the Koryu's primary weapon						
Options	• None						

KOHAI

Type	Rank	CP	Initiative	Fight	Shoot	Armour	Points
Koryu	3	3	3	3	2	None	20
Weapons	Special						
Attributes	Bujutsu for the Koryu's primary weapon						
Options	• None						

SENPAI

Type	Rank	CP	Initiative	Fight	Shoot	Armour	Points
Koryu	4	4	4	4	2	None	26
Weapons	Special						
Attributes	Commander, Bujutsu for the Koryu's primary weapon, and many choose one additional Attribute for +3 points						
Options	• None						

SENSEI

Type	Rank	CP	Initiative	Fight	Shoot	Armour	Points
Koryu	5	5	4	5	3	None	31
Weapons	Special						
Attributes	Commander, Bujutsu for the Koryu's primary weapon , and many choose up to two additional Attributes for +3 points each						
Options	• None						

Japanese wako raid a Chinese village, by Richard Hook © Osprey Publishing Ltd. Taken from Warrior 125: *Pirate of the Far East*.

BANDITS

'What? His sword? I exchanged it in town for liquor.' – Tajomaru the Bandit, *Rashomon*

BACKGROUND

During the almost constant warfare of the Sengoku Jidai there were plenty of opportunities for lawless bands of criminals, pirates, refugees and deserters to prey on the weak and defenceless. This faction represents the bandits that roamed the countryside or even the pirates (known as wako) that plagued shipping on the Sea of Japan. Some wako raids on Korea and China were virtually mini-invasions. As most of its equipment will be looted or stolen, a Bandit Buntai will have a highly irregular appearance. The Leader and his lieutenants will have the best arms and armour and may even pass for low-level Samurai, though they do not have the same fighting abilities. The rest of the Buntai have a mixture of weapons and armour.

Bandits would have come into conflict with all the other factions in *Ronin*, and no doubt could be found in Korea during the Imjin Wars as well. While not a strong faction, it is colourful and fun to play.

COMPOSITION

- There must be more Rank 0 and Rank 1 models than Rank 2 or higher.
- There may only be one Rank 3 model.
- No more than 10% of the models may be armed with a teppo, which may not be well maintained. On an Attack Roll of double 1 or double 2, the teppo becomes useless and may not be fired again this game.
- No more than 50% of the models may have a missile weapon.

SPECIAL RULES

This faction scores additional Victory Points for collecting loot. For every model that survives and was able to loot the body of enemy model of Rank 3 or higher, an additional 1 Victory Point is scored.

MORALE

The Morale Rating of Bandits is 7. If a Morale Test is failed, you may remove as a casualty any friendly model within 6" of the Leader to change the result to a pass.

SWORDS-FOR-HIRE

Bandits may hire Ronin.

MODEL LIST

PEASANT

Type	Rank	CP	Initiative	Fight	Shoot	Armour	Points
Peasant	0	1	1	1	0	None	4
Weapons	Improvised weapon						
Attributes	None						
Options	• May have yari for +4 points						

BANDIT

Type	Rank	CP	Initiative	Fight	Shoot	Armour	Points
Bandit	1	2	2	2	1	Light	13
Weapons	Katana						
Attributes	None						
Options	• May have one of yari, yumi or teppo for +3 points • May have medium armour for +2 point • May be fielded with no armour for -2 points						

GASHIRA

Type	Rank	CP	Initiative	Fight	Shoot	Armour	Points
Samurai	2	3	3	3	2	Light	20
Weapons	Katana						
Attributes	Commander and up to 50% of the Gashira in the Buntai may choose one additional Attribute for +3 points						
Options	• May have one of naginata, nodachi, yari, tetsubo, teppo or yumi for +3 points • May be mounted on a horse for +10 points • May have medium armour for +2 points • May be fielded with no armour for -2 points						

LEADER

Type	Rank	CP	Initiative	Fight	Shoot	Armour	Points
Samurai	3	3	3	3	2	Heavy	24
Weapons	Katana						
Attributes	Commander and may choose one additional Attribute for +3 points						
Options	• May have one of naginata, nodachi, yari, tetsubo, teppo or yumi for +3 points • May be mounted on a horse for +10 points • May exchange heavy armour for medium armour for -2 points • May be fielded with no armour for -6 points						

KOREANS

'The war is at its height – wear my armour and beat my war drums. Do not announce my death.' – Admiral Yi Sun-shin at the Battle of Noryang, 1598

BACKGROUND

Korea was the only foreign country ever to be invaded by the Samurai armies of Japan in a brutal war which caused unimaginable suffering and hardship for the Korean people. Korea was at that time a vassal state of Ming China, and although it had a large standing army, it was poorly trained, disorganised and ineptly led. Consequently, the Koreans were systematically defeated by the battle-hardened Japanese in almost every major battle. However, the Koreans did mount an effective guerrilla war against the Japanese and large parts of the country remained in Korean hands, even if many major cities and fortresses were captured. The Korean navy was considerably more successful and inflicted a lot of damage on Japanese transports and troop ships, disrupting supplies and reinforcements.

Korean foot soldiers were unarmoured and, although brave, were no match for the armoured Bushi. The Koreans did appear to have had better-equipped heavy infantry and cavalry, but these troop types were relatively scarce. Many Korean monks also took up arms against the invaders. The Koreans have a good selection of troops but suffer from poor Morale.

COMPOSITION

- There must be more Rank 0 and 1 models than Rank 3 or 4 models.
- There may be no more than one Rank 2 model for every four Rank 0 or Rank 1 models.
- There may only be one Rank 4 model.
- No more than 10% of the models may be armed with an arquebus and no more than 50% of the models may have a missile weapon.
- If Monks are fielded, then no Heavy Cavalry or Heavy Infantry may be used.

SPECIAL RULES

Koreans score one additional Victory Point for each Samurai model that is killed.

Some Korean models may be armed with a flail, which adds +2 to the Attack Roll but -1 to Initiative.

One Korean Soldier or Monk may be equipped with a banner for no cost. This Model may not have any additional equipment.

MORALE

The Morale Rating of Koreans is 7.

SWORDS-FOR-HIRE

No Swords-for-Hire may be selected.

MODEL LIST

PEASANT

Type	Rank	CP	Initiative	Fight	Shoot	Armour	Points
Peasant	0	1	1	1	0	None	4
Weapons	Improvised weapon						
Attributes	None						
Options	• None						

SOLDIER

Type	Rank	CP	Initiative	Fight	Shoot	Armour	Points
Soldier	1	2	2	2	1	None	11
Weapons	Sword						
Attributes	None						
Options	• May have one of spear, arquebus or bow for +3 points						

MONK

Type	Rank	CP	Initiative	Fight	Shoot	Armour	Points
Monk	1	2	2	2	1	None	13
Weapons	Sword						
Attributes	Fearless						
Options	• May have one of spear, arquebus or bow for +3 points						

CAPTAIN

Type	Rank	CP	Initiative	Fight	Shoot	Armour	Points
Soldier	2	2	2	3	1	None	14
Weapons	Sword						
Attributes	Commander						
Options	• May have one of spear or bow for +3 points • May have shield (light armour) for +1 point						

HEAVY INFANTRY

Type	Rank	CP	Initiative	Fight	Shoot	Armour	Points
Soldier	3	3	3	3	2	Heavy	23
Weapons	Sword and shield						
Attributes	May choose one Attribute for +3 points						
Options	• May exchange shield (armour becomes medium) for one of bow, spear or halberd for +3 points • May exchange shield (armour becomes medium) for an additional sword (Combat Pool increases to 4) for no cost						

HEAVY CAVALRY

Type	Rank	CP	Initiative	Fight	Shoot	Armour	Points
Soldier	3	3	3	3	2	Medium	31
Weapons	Sword and horse						
Attributes	May choose one Attribute for +3 points						
Options	• May have one of flail or bow for +3 points • May have an additional sword (Combat Pool increases to 4) for +3 points						

COMMANDER

Type	Rank	CP	Initiative	Fight	Shoot	Armour	Points
Soldier	4	4	3	4	2	Heavy	28
Weapons	Sword and shield						
Attributes	Commander and may choose up to two additional Attributes for +3 points each						
Options	• May exchange shield (armour becomes medium) for one of bow, spear or halberd for +3 points • May exchange shield (armour becomes medium) for an additional sword (Combat Pool increases to 5) for no cost. • May be mounted on a horse for +10 points						

MING CHINESE

'The opportunity to secure ourselves against defeat lies in our own hands, but the opportunity of defeating the enemy is provided by the enemy himself.' – Sun Tzu

BACKGROUND

Even before the Japanese invasion of Korea, the Ming Chinese were accustomed to Japanese aggression. Large-scale pirate raids often targeted the Chinese mainland, some so large that they almost amounted to mini-invasions. When the Japanese invaded Korea in 1592, the Ming government was distracted by two separate rebellions elsewhere and was subsequently slow to react. It was almost three months before the first Chinese forces marched into Korea, and another 6 months of bitter fighting before the Japanese began to be driven back. A second Japanese invasion in 1597 initially regained lost ground, but the combined might of China and Korea was eventually too much for the outnumbered Japanese.

The Ming Chinese were well-armed and well-led. They had access to firearms as well as cannon, and could draw upon bow-armed steppe cavalry. This is a strong faction and a good match for Bushi.

Ming troops, by Christa Hook © Osprey Publishing Ltd. Taken from Men-at-Arms 307: *Late Imperial Chinese Armies 1520–1840.*

COMPOSITION

- There must be more Rank 0 and Rank 1 models than Rank 3 or 4 models.
- There may be no more than one Rank 2 model for every four Rank 0 or Rank 1 models.
- There may only be one Rank 4 model.
- No more than 25% of the models may be armed with an arquebus, and no more than 50% of the models may have a missile weapon.

SPECIAL RULES

One Soldier may be equipped with a banner for no cost. This model may not have any additional equipment.

MORALE

The Morale Rating of Ming Chinese is 9.

SWORDS-FOR-HIRE

No Swords-for-Hire may be selected.

MODEL LIST

SOLDIER

Type	Rank	CP	Initiative	Fight	Shoot	Armour	Points
Soldier	1	2	2	2	1	Medium	15
Weapons	Sword						
Attributes	None						
Options	• May have one of spear, arquebus or bow for +3 points						

LIGHT CAVALRY

Type	Rank	CP	Initiative	Fight	Shoot	Armour	Points
Soldier	1	2	2	2	2	None	28
Weapons	Sword, bow and horse						
Attributes	Bajutsu						
Options	• None						

CAPTAIN

Type	Rank	CP	Initiative	Fight	Shoot	Armour	Points
Soldier	2	2	2	3	1	Medium	18
Weapons	Sword and shield						
Attributes	Commander						
Options	• May have one of spear or bow for +3 points						

HEAVY INFANTRY

Type	Rank	CP	Initiative	Fight	Shoot	Armour	Points
Soldier	3	3	3	3	2	Heavy	23
Weapons	Sword and shield						
Attributes	May choose one Attribute for +3 points						
Options	• May exchange shield (armour becomes medium) for one of bow, spear or halberd for +3 points • May exchange shield (armour becomes medium) for an additional sword (Combat Pool increases to 4) for no cost						

HEAVY CAVALRY

Type	Rank	CP	Initiative	Fight	Shoot	Armour	Points
Soldier	3	3	3	3	2	Medium	34
Weapons	Sword, spear and horse						
Attributes	May choose one Attribute for +3 points						
Options	• None						

COMMANDER

Type	Rank	CP	Initiative	Fight	Shoot	Armour	Points
Soldier	4	4	3	4	2	Heavy	28
Weapons	Sword and shield						
Attributes	Commander and may choose up to two additional Attributes for +3 points each						
Options	• May exchange shield (armour becomes medium) for one of bow, spear or halberd for +3 points • May be mounted on a horse for +10 points						

PEASANTS

'What do you think of farmers? You think they're saints? Hah! They're foxy beasts!' – Kikuchiyo, *Seven Samurai*

BACKGROUND

Common farmers would often be caught up the wars of this time, usually coming off second-best. The classic film *Seven Samurai* tells the story of a group of peasants who fight back, hiring ronin to assist them. This final Buntai is not particularly powerful, but has plenty of character!

COMPOSITION

- At least 30% of points must be spent on Peasants.

SPECIAL RULES

This Buntai scores additional Victory Points for collecting loot. For every model that survives and was able to loot the body of an enemy model of Rank 1 or 2, an additional ½ Victory Point is scored. Each model that survives and has looted an enemy model of Rank 3 or higher earns his Buntai an additional 1 Victory Point.

MORALE

The Morale Rating of Peasants is dependent on the degree to which they outnumber the enemy Buntai. If the ratio of Peasant models to enemy models is at least 3:1, then Peasant Morale is 8. If it is less than 3:1 but more than 2:1, then Morale is 7. If it is less than 2:1, it is 6.

SWORDS-FOR-HIRE

Any number of Ronin and/or up to one Warrior Monk or Shugyosha may be hired.

MODEL LIST

PEASANT

Type	Rank	CP	Initiative	Fight	Shoot	Armour	Points
Peasant	0	1	1	1	0	None	4
Weapons	Improvised weapon						
Attributes	None						
Options	• May have yari for +4 points						

SWORDS-FOR-HIRE

'Even bears come out of the woods when they're hungry' – villager, *Seven Samurai*

The models in this section may join certain Buntai as individuals or in small groups. These models will not be subject to any special scoring rules and are not counted when determining Buntai composition.

RONIN

Ronin were masterless Samurai, often down on their luck. They roamed Japan during the Sengoku Jidai as mercenaries, bodyguards and, occasionally, bandits.

SPECIAL RULES

Ronin are unreliable. If the Morale level of the Buntai is Wavering, roll a d6 for each Ronin. On a roll of 4+, that Ronin model will use its activation to move at maximum speed towards the nearest table edge until it has left the table. If it is in combat, it will Withdraw. If the Morale of the Buntai drops to Routing, Ronin will automatically follow the procedure described above. You may only ever field one Senior Ronin and only if you have already selected at least two other Ronin.

RONIN

Type	Rank	CP	Initiative	Fight	Shoot	Armour	Points
Samurai	3	3	3	3	2	None	17
Weapons	Katana and wakizashi						
Attributes	May choose up to two Attributes for +3 points each						
Options	• May have one of naginata, nodachi, yari, tetsubo, teppo or yumi for +3 points • May have light armour for +2 points • May have medium armour for +4 points • May have heavy armour for +6 points						

SENIOR RONIN

Type	Rank	CP	Initiative	Fight	Shoot	Armour	Points
Samurai	4	4	4	4	2	None	22
Weapons	Katana and wakizashi						
Attributes	Commander and may choose up to three additional Attributes for +3 points each						
Options	• May have one of naginata, nodachi, yari, tetsubo, teppo or yumi for +3 points • May have light armour for +2 points • May have medium armour for +4 points • May have heavy armour for +6 points						

WARRIOR MONK

The warrior monks of Japan fought for and against the Samurai and Ikko-Ikki. One of the most famous of these was Benkei, who lived in the 12th century and became the companion and bodyguard of the Samurai Minamoto no Yoshitsune. Warrior monks were famous for their use of the Naginata.

SPECIAL RULES

Sohei are Fearless and so never check Morale.

WARRIOR MONK

Type	Rank	CP	Initiative	Fight	Shoot	Armour	Points
Sohei	3	3	3	3	2	Medium	26
Weapons	Katana and one of naginata, tetsubo or yumi						
Attributes	Fearless and may choose up to two additional Attributes for +3 points each						
Options	• May be fielded with no armour for -4 points						

SHUGYOSHA

Great martial artists such as Miyamato Musashi could be found wandering throughout Japan during this period, testing their skills against other warriors, gathering disciples or seeking enlightenment. These men were known as shugyosha. Some would dress simply, almost as beggars, while others would wear flashy clothes and loudly proclaim their martial virtues wherever they went. Sometimes these individuals would lend their skills to a particular fight. You may only ever field one Shugyosha.

SHUGYOSHA

Type	Rank	CP	Initiative	Fight	Shoot	Armour	Points
Shugyosha	5	5	4	5	3	None	28
Weapons	Katana						
Attributes	Commander and may choose up to four additional Attributes for +3 points each						
Options	• May exchange katana for jo, bo or kasurigama at no cost • May exchange katana for naginata, nodachi or tetsubo for +3 points						

NINJA

Ninja were spies, saboteurs and assassins. Although popular culture depicts them dressed in black, in reality they would have taken on any guise necessary to fulfil their mission. So if you field a Ninja, it can take the form of a specific model in your Buntai, leaving your opponent guessing as to who it is!

SPECIAL RULES

You may only ever field one Ninja, but you do have the option of fielding it as disguised or undisguised. If you are fielding an undisguised Ninja, then use the profile below. After both sides have deployed, you may place the Ninja model anywhere on the board, provided it is not within 6" of an enemy model.

If you are fielding a disguised Ninja, then it will take the place of a Rank 0 or 1 model of your choice and will be deployed with the rest of your Buntai. You do not need a special model for a disguised Ninja – it will appear exactly as a normal model of that type. Before the game starts, you must declare that you are fielding a Ninja and set aside a piece of paper with a description of which model is the Ninja. Of course, you may also choose to declare that you are fielding a Ninja even if you are not, just to give your opponent some food for thought! However, this will earn you a -1 Victory Point penalty at the end of the game. You may choose to conceal the Ninja's identity for as long as you wish, even to the extent of under-representing the Combat Pool and Fight Characteristic of the Ninja in combat. You can at any point declare the presence of the Ninja, confirming this fact by showing the note you had written before the game. If the Ninja is in combat with any model at the moment of its declaration, the opposing model (or models) immediately loses one counter from its Combat Pool of your choice.

UNDISGUISED NINJA

Type	Rank	CP	Initiative	Fight	Shoot	Armour	Points
Ninja	3	3	3	3	2	Light	26
Weapons	Katana and shuriken						
Attributes	Acrobatic and one Bujutsu						
Options	• May exchange katana for kasurigama at no cost						

DISGUISED NINJA

Type	Rank	CP	Initiative	Fight	Shoot	Armour	Points
Ninja	3	3	3	3	2	As model	26
Weapons	Shuriken and all the equipment of the model it is impersonating						
Attributes	Acrobatic and one Bujutsu						
Options	• None						

A SAMPLE BUNTAI

A player decides to build a Bushi Buntai starting at 100 points, which he will later expand. His first selection is an Ashigaru armed with a teppo for 18 points. He then adds an Ashigaru with yumi for another 18 and two

Ashigaru with yari for 36 points. He has 28 points left and so selects a Samurai with Kenjutsu for 27 points, who is also a logical leader for his Buntai. His Buntai consists of the following models:

- 1 Ashigaru with teppo – 18 points
- 1 Ashigaru with yumi – 18 points
- 2 Ashigaru with yari – 36 points (18 points each)
- 1 Samurai with Kenjutsu – 27 points
- Total – 99 points

To expand his small force up to 200 points, he decides to add a Hatamoto with naginata, Naginatajutsu and the Powerful Ability, and a Samurai with yari and Sojutsu. These expensive but potent models come in at a total of 65 points. To add some additional support, and to make the list conform to its composition rules, he includes another two ashigaru – one with a teppo and one with a yumi – for another 36 points.

- 2 Ashigaru with teppo – 36 points (18 points each)
- 2 Ashigaru with yumi – 36 points (18 points each)
- 2 Ashigaru with yari – 36 points (18 points each)
- 1 Samurai with Kenjutsu – 27 points
- 1 Samurai with yari and Sojutsu – 30 points
- 1 Hatamoto with naginata, Naginatajutsu and Powerful – 35 points
- Total – 200 points

SCENARIOS

SETTING UP THE GAME

PLAYING AREA

The size of an ideal playing area for a 100-point game of *Ronin* is 24"x24". For larger games of between 100 and 200 points, a playing area of 36"x36" is recommended. For very large games of more than 200 points, at least 48"x48" is recommended.

TERRAIN

Terrain is an important part of *Ronin*, providing cover for models and defining the battlefield. It also looks good, vastly adding to the aesthetic enjoyment of the game. Each scenario has recommendations for the terrain to be used and there are rules for the placement of this terrain. However, many players prefer to simply randomly put some terrain on the table and then get playing, and this is a perfectly acceptable approach.

RANDOM TERRAIN PLACEMENT

1. First, determine the location of the battle and therefore the type of terrain by rolling on the following table:

D6 roll	Location of Battle	Terrain Examples
1	Urban	Houses, walls, gardens
2–3	Rural	Fields, rice paddies, farmhouses, streams
4–5	Wilderness	Forests, marshes, hills, rivers
6	Mixed	Roll twice more, ignoring further rolls of 6, and split the terrain evenly between the two results

2. Next, determine the number of terrain pieces: d3+3 for a game up to 200 points in size and d3+5 for game of more than 200 points.
3. The size of the terrain pieces is determined as follows. Small terrain pieces are anything smaller than 6" in diameter, whilst large pieces are up to 12" in diameter. The size of terrain pieces is going to vary considerably, so use your discretion on how you decide to classify it.

Total number of terrain pieces	Number of large terrain pieces	Number of small terrain pieces
4	1	3
5	2	3
6	2	4
7	3	4
8	3	5

4. Terrain is then placed randomly by dividing the playing area into quarters. Both players roll a d6 (re-rolling draws) and the player with the highest score places one piece of terrain in each of three different quarters of his choice. The second player may then move two of these terrain pieces by up to 6". The second player then places the next three pieces, again no more than one to a quarter, and the first player may then move two of these new pieces by up to 6". Finally, the first player places any remaining terrain, again no more than one per quarter, and the second player may move up to two of these by up to 6".

WEATHER

Some scenarios will be affected by different types of weather. If you decide to use weather, roll a d6 and consult the table below:

D6 roll	Weather	Effect
1–2	Heavy Mist	Line of sight is reduced to 12"
3–4	Rain	Line of sight is reduced to 24". Teppo may only be fired once
5–6	Wind	All yumi suffer an additional -1 penalty on Attack Rolls

TIME OF DAY

Not all battles take place during the day. If you wish to change the time of day, roll a d6 and consult the table below:

D6 roll	Time of Day	Effect
1–2	Night	Line of sight is reduced to 12"
3–4	Dusk	Line of sight is reduced to 18" in Turn 3 and to 12" from Turn 4 onwards
5–6	Dawn	Line of sight is 18" in Turn 1 and 2, and unrestricted thereafter

VICTORY POINTS

The winner of a battle will be determined by the number of Victory Points that are earned. Some Factions and scenarios have special Victory Point conditions, but these general rules apply to most scenarios:

- Each side gains Victory Points equal to the Rank of each enemy model killed (Rank 0 Models are worth 0.5 points each).
- Captured enemy Banners are worth 5 Victory Points.
- Each enemy model that has Routed and left the table is worth Victory Points equal to half its Rank.

DEPLOYMENT RULES

There are a number of different deployment options.

- Edges – Once terrain has been placed, both players roll a d6. The player with the highest roll selects one table edge and deploys his figures up to 2" in from that edge. The second player then does likewise on the opposite edge.
- Corners – Once terrain has been placed, both players roll a d6. The player with the highest roll selects one table corner and deploys his figures up to 6" in from that corner. The second player then does likewise on the opposite corner.
- Reserves – If the Reserves rule is used, then each player may only deploy half of his models (rounding up), with the other half being kept off-table. Half of these reserve models (rounding up) may move onto the table during the Move Phase of the second turn. All remaining models may move onto the table during the Move Phase of the third turn.

SKIRMISH

SCENARIO DESCRIPTION

In this generic scenario, two forces of equal size meet and fight a battle.

SCENARIO RULES

- Forces: Both sides select a force of equal points value.
- Terrain: Use the standard terrain placement rules.
- Weather: Roll a d6. On a 5 or 6, roll again on the weather table. Otherwise, the weather will have no effect on the game.
- Time of Day: Roll a d6. On a 6, roll again on the time of day table. Otherwise the engagement takes place during daylight hours.
- Deployment: Both players roll a d6. The player who rolls highest chooses either Edge or Corner deployment. Reserves may be used if both players agree.

VICTORY POINTS

Standard Victory Points are used. Additionally, each side must roll on the following table to determine a minor objective. Achieving this Minor Objective is worth 5 Victory Points.

D6 roll	Minor Objective
1	Capture any enemy model of at least Rank 2
2	Control the table by having the most models in each table quarter
3	Kill the enemy Leader
4	Lose no more than 25% of your force
5	Kill more than 75% of the enemy Buntai
6	Same Minor Objective as opponent. If both players roll a 6, neither has a Minor Objective.

GAME LENGTH

The game lasts for d6+6 turns (determined at the start of the game) or until one side withdraws, concedes or is destroyed.

CAPTURE

SCENARIO DESCRIPTION

In this scenario both sides attempt to take control of an objective. This may be a religious artefact, the body of a slain commander, a treasure trove or something of equivalent value that is worth fighting over.

SCENARIO RULES

- Forces: Both sides select a force of equal points value.
- Terrain: Use the standard terrain placement rules. The objective must be placed in the exact centre of the board, inside or on top of any terrain that may be present.
- Weather: Roll a d6. On a 5 or 6, roll again on the weather table. Otherwise, the weather will have no effect on the game.
- Time of Day: Roll a d6. On a 6, roll again on the time of day table. Otherwise the engagement takes place during daylight hours.
- Deployment: Edge deployment. Reserves are not used.

VICTORY POINTS

Both sides are attempting to take control of the objective, which counts as a heavy object. To count as having control, a model must be in base-to-base contact with the objective and not be engaged or two friendly models must be carrying the objective and not be engaged. If one side controls the objective at the end of the game (or has been able to remove it from the board), it gains an additional 5 Victory Points.

GAME LENGTH

The game lasts for 8 turns.

DUEL

SCENARIO DESCRIPTION

Duels were common in Japan during this period, and ranged from highly formal pre-arranged affairs between two individuals to spontaneous brawls. This scenario represents such a duel, initially between just two models, but eventually the entire Buntai will be drawn in.

SCENARIO RULES

- Forces: Both sides select a force of equal points value.
- Terrain: Use the standard terrain placement rules, except that a 12" circular area in the middle of the table must be left clear of all terrain.
- Weather: Roll a d6. On a 5 or 6, roll again on the weather table. Otherwise, the weather will have no effect on the game.
- Time of Day: Roll a d6. On a 6, roll again on the time of day table. Otherwise the engagement takes place during daylight hours.
- Deployment: Roll a d6. The player who rolls highest places his nominated duellist (see below) at some point on the edge of the duelling area and the rest of his models within 6" of the duellist but not within the duelling area. The other player follows the same procedure. Roll a d6 once more to see which player goes first.

VICTORY POINTS

Standard Victory Points are used, along with the special modifiers below.

GAME LENGTH

The game lasts for d6+6 turns or until one side withdraws, concedes or is destroyed.

SPECIAL RULE: DUELLISTS

At the start of the game, each player nominates one model from his Buntai to be his duellist. The duellists from each side will initially be the only models allowed inside the duelling area and will be the only models that fight. If a duellist is critically injured, another model can be nominated to replace it and may use its next movement to enter the duelling area. This model is now considered a duellist.

For the first 2 turns, only the duellists may be activated and they may not use any missile weapons. All other models must remain where they are deployed. From Turn 3, all models may be activated as normal.

Certain actions will count as negative Victory Points. The first non-duellist model to attack another model (either in hand-to-hand or with shooting, whether successful or not) will incur -2 Victory Points. The first non-duellist model that enters the duelling area will incur -2 Victory Points.

DEFENCE

SCENARIO DESCRIPTION

In this scenario, one side attempts to defend a strategic point at any cost. This may be a shrine, a hill, a building or something similar. The attacking side gets twice as many points as the defending side, and must wrest control of the objective.

SCENARIO RULES

- Forces: Determine which side is attacking and which side is defending (roll randomly if necessary). The Attacker has twice as many points as the Defender.
- Terrain: Use the standard terrain placement rules. However, a small piece of terrain that will act as the objective must be placed in the centre of the table, and no other terrain piece may be within 8" of this. This terrain piece must be substantial enough to provide heavy cover.

- Weather: Roll a d6. On a 5 or 6, roll again on the weather table. Otherwise, the weather will have no effect on the game.
- Time of Day: Roll a d6. On a 6, roll again on the time of day table. Otherwise the engagement takes place during daylight hours.
- Deployment: The defending side deploys first and must place all of its models within 12" of the objective. The Defender then nominates the table edge along which the Attacker will deploy. The Attacker uses the Reserves rule.

VICTORY POINTS

Standard Victory Points are used. Additionally, the side that controls the objective gets an additional 10 Victory Points.

GAME LENGTH

The game lasts for d6+6 turns or until one side withdraws, concedes or is destroyed.

ASSASSINATION

SCENARIO DESCRIPTION

In this scenario, one side attempts to foil an assassination attempt by a group of Ninja controlled by the other.

SCENARIO RULES

- Forces: The defending player selects 150 points of models. The attacking player fields 1 Chunin and 5 Ninja, using the profiles provided below.
- Terrain: Once the location of the battle and number of terrain pieces are determined, the attacking player deploys all of the terrain. The defending player may then move half of the terrain pieces by up to 6".
- Weather: Roll a d6. On a 5 or 6, roll again on the weather table. Otherwise, the weather will have no effect on the game. The Attacking player may choose to re-roll the initial roll OR the roll on the weather table, but must abide by the second roll.
- Time of Day: Roll a d6. On a 6, roll again on the time of day table. Otherwise the engagement takes place during daylight hours. The Attacking player may choose to re-roll the initial roll OR the roll on the time of day table, but must abide by the second roll.
- Deployment: This game is played on a 36" square table. The attacking player deploys all of the defending players' models within 12" of the centre of the table, and then all of his own models anywhere on the table, but no nearer than 9" to any of the defending player's models. The defending player may then move no more than half of his models up to 6". Finally, the attacking player may re-deploy two of his models anywhere he wishes.

VICTORY POINTS

The Attacker's objective is to kill the Defender's Leader – the Defender's objective is to prevent this. No other scoring criteria are used.

GAME LENGTH

The game lasts for d6+6 turns or until one side withdraws, concedes or is destroyed.

SPECIAL RULE: NINJA

The attacking player uses the following profiles for his Buntai of 1 Chunin and 5 Ninja. The attacking player automatically wins priority on the first turn. Ninja do not have to check Morale.

NINJA

Type	Rank	CP	Initiative	Fight	Shoot	Armour	Points
Ninja	3	3	3	3	2	Light	n/a
Weapons	Katana and shuriken						
Attributes	Acrobatic and Kenjutsu						

CHUNIN

Type	Rank	CP	Initiative	Fight	Shoot	Armour	Points
Ninja	4	4	3	4	2	Light	n/a
Weapons	Katana and shuriken						
Attributes	Acrobatic and Kenjutsu						

TOURNAMENT

SCENARIO DESCRIPTION

In this scenario, two Buntai fight a series of formal matches to determine which is the stronger. This is a special type of scenario, as only two models will ever be fighting at one time, and terrain does not play a part. The tournament may take place in a large room, the courtyard of a fortress or a clearing in a wilderness setting.

SCENARIO RULES

- Forces: This scenario does not use points. Both players agree on the number of models and the ranks of the models that will participate in the tournament. These models may then be equipped in any way that is permitted by their lists.
- Terrain: This scenario does not require terrain except for aesthetics. All that is required is a 12" circular duelling area.
- Weather: The weather is fine, there is no need to roll.
- Time of Day: This engagement takes place during daylight hours or inside a well-lit building.
- Deployment: Deployment is not used.

VICTORY POINTS

No Victory Points are used – see Special Rule: The Tournament, below.

GAME LENGTH

The game lasts until one side withdraws, concedes or is destroyed.

SPECIAL RULE: THE TOURNAMENT

Each player secretly records the order in which his models will fight. When both players have done this, the first model from each side will fight a match. Each match lasts for 6 turns, or until one model is killed. At the end of 6 turns, if both models are still alive, the winner is the model that has scored the most match points, where a Light wound is worth 1 match point, a Grievous wound is worth 2 and a Critical wound is worth 3. If both models have the same number of match points or none were scored, the match is draw.

The winner of the scenario is the side that won the most matches. If both sides are equal, the winner is the side that scored the most match points. If this is also equal, the two highest ranking surviving models on each side fight another match, with no time limit. The winner of this final match is the winner of the tournament.

Ninja assault a castle, by Wayne Reynolds
© Osprey Publishing Ltd. Taken from Warrior 64: *Ninja AD 1460–1650*

DEFEND THE VILLAGE

SCENARIO DESCRIPTION
In this scenario, one Buntai is tasked with defending a group of civilians from the other Buntai. These civilians are mostly helpless, but some will show some fight if attacked by the enemy.

SCENARIO RULES
* Forces: Both sides select a force of equal points value. For every 25 points, one civilian model is required. Roll a d6 to determine which side is the Attacker and which side is the Defender.
* Terrain: The Defender places the terrain. At least one building is ideal.
* Weather: Roll a d6. On a 5 or 6, roll again on the weather table. Otherwise, the weather will have no effect on the game.
* Time of Day: Roll a d6. On a 6, roll again on the time of day table. Otherwise the engagement takes place during daylight hours.
* Deployment: The Defender deploys his entire force first, along with the civilians, anywhere on the table. The Attacker then deploys his entire force anywhere within 3" of a table edge (models do not necessarily have to be grouped together).

VICTORY POINTS

Standard Victory Points are used. In addition, for each civilian model left on the board at the end of the game the Defender gains +3 Victory Points. For each civilian slain, the Attacker gains +3 Victory Points.

GAME LENGTH

The game lasts until one side withdraws, concedes or is destroyed.

SPECIAL RULE: CIVILIANS

Civilian models will not deliberately engage an enemy model in combat. If a civilian model is engaged, roll a d6. On a result of 1–3, the civilian is considered to have a Fight and Combat Pool of 0. On a 4–6, the civilian has the Characteristics below:

Type	Rank	CP	Initiative	Fight	Shoot	Armour	Points
Peasant	0	1	1	1	0	None	n/a
Weapons	Improvised weapon						
Attributes	None						

Civilians many move up to 6" in the Move Phase if there is friendly model within 6" of them, but they may not leave the board.

CAMPAIGNS

Campaigns add a lot of enjoyment to wargaming. This brief campaign system allows two players to play a number of linked games.

Each player builds a master roster up to an agreed number of points – 300, for example. Each player must then secretly prepare three small Buntai, using only models from the master roster. Normal composition rules may be ignored for the small Buntai, but not the master roster. Each small Buntai must be between 25% and 50% of the total points cost of the master roster. Each player then secretly assigns one of these Buntai to one of the following scenarios – Skirmish, Capture and Defend. Players then play each of these scenarios, recording the models that are killed and wounded.

All surviving models on both sides then compete in another Skirmish battle to determine the winner of the campaign. Models that end their initial game with a Light wound may be used in the final battle. Models that suffer a Grievous wound are only available on a roll of 4+ on a d6.

PROGRESSION

If you have regular games against the same opponents, you may decide to allow progression, where models gain experience in battle and develop their skills, eventually increasing in Rank. Some of the greatest warriors of this period began life as lowly Ashigaru.

All models start with 0 Experience. Experience is gained in the following way:

- Surviving a battle: +1
- Inflicting a Light wound (or worse) on an enemy model of equal or greater Rank: +1
- Capturing a banner: +1

Models may then spend Experience to progress to the next Rank. The cost of progressing from one Rank to the next is as follows:

- Rank 0 to Rank 1:
  5 points
- Rank 1 to Rank 2:
  5 points
- Rank 2 to Rank 3:
  5 points
- Rank 3 to Rank 4:
  10 points
- Rank 4 to Rank 5:
  15 points

Models that go up a Rank automatically gain the Attributes and options available to their new Rank. All existing Attributes are retained. This may lead to a model having more Attributes than a model of similar Rank.

Progression is not mandatory – you may choose to leave a model at the same Rank.

With most factions, movement from one Rank to the next is obvious. Bushi, for example, only have one type of model of each Rank. The exceptions are detailed below:

- Ikko-Ikki: a Monto may progress to become a Sohei, but a Sohei will progress to become a Senior Sohei (as detailed under the Sohei Faction) and then to a Grandmaster.
- Koreans: a Captain may choose to progress to become either Heavy Cavalry or Heavy Infantry.
- Ming Chinese: a Captain may choose to progress to become either Heavy Cavalry or Heavy Infantry. Only a Soldier equipped with a bow may progress to become Light Cavalry, and this model must gain enough Experience to jump two levels before it progresses again, when it will become Heavy Cavalry.

TOURNAMENTS

Tournaments are a good way to play a number of games in one day against different opponents and forces. The standard format is the well-known Swiss Draw system, where players are randomly decided in the first round and then allocated against opponents with a similar win/loss ratio from there on. Performance in any *Ronin* tournament should be decided on the number of wins, with accrued Victory Points used as a tie-breaker.

More adventurous tournament organisers may like to try a different method by requiring each player to submit an army that is substantially larger than the game sizes, and then manage the casualties suffered throughout the course of the tournament. For example, for a 150-point tournament players may be allowed to bring a 400-point roster, and select 150 points of models from it at the beginning of each game. The composition of the roster must comply with the composition rules for the faction. The compositions of each 150-point Buntai must also comply with the composition rules as closely as possible, though the wounds suffered by models during the games may make this impossible (see below). In this situation, each Buntai must align with the composition rules as closely as possible. Models that end each game with wounds may not be available for the next. Models with Stunned counters or Light wounds are considered healthy again for the next game, but Models that suffer a Grievous wound must 'rest' for one game, after which they are considered back to full heath again. Models that are slain are no longer available.

ADVANCED RULES

The following rules add an extra level of complexity and record-keeping to the game of *Ronin*, so not all players may wish to use them. They do, however, add an extra dimension to the game and so are included here as optional advanced rules.

FATIGUE

Combat is an exhausting experience, more so than all other activities, and may lead to a model becoming fatigued.

To use Fatigue, each model gains an extra Characteristic called Resilience. The Resilience Characteristic of all models of Rank 0, 1 and 2 is 7; Rank 3 and 4 models have a Resilience of 8; and Rank 5 models have a Resilience of 9.

Fatigue is checked in the End Phase after Stunned counters are removed, in the order described below:

1. Remove Fatigue counters: Each model that did not fight in combat this turn and has at least one Fatigue counter may remove d3 Fatigue Counters.
2. Check for Fatigue: For each model that did fight in combat this turn, roll 2d6 and compare the sum of the two dice with the model's Resilience Characteristic. If this number is lower than or equal to the Resilience of that model, it has passed its Resilience Test for this turn and suffers no ill effects. However, if the result is higher, the model gains a Fatigue counter. The following modifiers apply to this roll:
   o Model already has at least one Fatigue counter: +1
   o Model has a Grievous wound: +1
   o Model Rested during the Action Phase: -2

A model that has at least one Fatigue counter is Fatigued, and suffers -1 to its Initiative and Shoot Characteristics.

NEW ATTRIBUTE: TIRELESS

If you decide to use Fatigue in your games, then include this new Attribute. Models with Tireless do not accumulate Fatigue.

APPENDIX – OTHER PERIODS

This appendix provides some brief guidelines on using *Ronin* to wargame other key periods of Japanese history. While not full-blown lists, there is sufficient information to play these periods. As with the main game, players are encouraged to come up with their own rules and variations.

KAMAKURA PERIOD

The most significant events of the Kamakura Period of Japanese history (roughly 1185–1330 AD) were the two Mongol invasions in 1274 and 1281. The Mongol emperor Kublai Khan had already subjugated the Korean peninsula and sent a number of envoys to Japan in the late 1260s to demand that it became a vassal state. Not unexpectedly, the Japanese refused, leading to the first Mongol invasion in 1274. The Mongol armies initially made significant progress against the Samurai, but made the catastrophic decision to re-embark their army to ride out a large storm. Many of their ships were sunk along with a large proportion of their army, and they were eventually forced to withdraw. The Japanese were much better prepared for the second invasion in 1281, having reorganised their forces and fortified sections of the coast. The Mongols made little progress this time before a massive typhoon almost completely destroyed their fleet.

The Samurai of this period favoured the bow over other weapons and, in melee, sought single combat whenever possible. The Mongols, on the other hand, had advanced tactics and exotic weapons such as hand grenades. There was no faulting the bravery of the Japanese, who even resorted to rowing out to the Mongol fleet in small fishing boats to attempt desperate and often suicidal boarding missions.

FACTIONS

BUSHI

The existing Bushi list may be used for the Japanese of this period, with the following adjustments:

- All Samurai may only be equipped with medium armour, resulting in a points adjustment of -2.
- Samurai must select Kyujutsu or Bajutsu before any other attribute is selected.
- Two Samurai may not combine to engage a single enemy model.
- Teppo may not be selected.
- Ashigaru (called Retainers in this period) may only be equipped with light armour, resulting in a points adjustment of -2.
- Ninja may not be selected as Swords-for-Hire.

MONGOLS

The Mongol army was very diverse, including both Korean and Chinese troops. The Mongols may use any models from the Ming Chinese list as well as Soldiers and Captains from the Korean list. The following adjustments apply:

- The Morale Rating of the Mongols is 9.
- No models may be equipped with arquebus, but models that could normally be equipped with arquebus may be equipped with a single grenade for the same points cost.

Special Rules: The Mongols used an early version of a grenade – an earthenware pot packed with gunpowder and shrapnel. Grenades have a range of just 6" and can only be used once. To use a grenade, the attacker selects a target point and then makes a standard Shooting Attack against that location (which obviously does not have any armour, though it may be in cover). If the attack is unsuccessful, the fuse of the grenade has gone out or something else has gone wrong and there is no effect. If the attack is successful, then all models that are at least partially within 2" of the target point must roll a d6 and add their armour modifier to the result (light +1, medium +2, heavy +3). Subtract the resulting score from 7 and refer to the Wound Table to see if a wound has been suffered.

BANDITS

The existing Bandit list may be used, but no teppo or heavy armour may be selected.

SOHEI

The existing Sohei list may be used, but no teppo may be selected.

LATE EDO PERIOD

The end of the 19th century saw massive changes in Japanese society. After centuries of self-imposed isolation, the country was forced to open up to

the outside after the intervention of an American warship. The Shogunate began to slowly disintegrate and the country was rocked by two significant civil wars – the Boshin War and the Satsuma Rebellion. These conflicts saw traditional Bushi fight with and against European-trained rifle-armed infantry, and in at least one case a Westerner donned Samurai armour and fought alongside the Japanese (though he was French, not American!).

SPECIAL RULES

REVOLVER

A revolver has a maximum range of 12", and suffers a -1 penalty to hit for distances over 6". However, like a yumi it can be fired repeatedly and models that are targeted by a revolver treat their armour as one class worse (heavy armour is considered medium, and so on).

RIFLE

From the 1840s modern firearms began to be imported into Japan, replacing the outdated matchlock teppos. Rifles may be fired every turn (but only once) whether the model moves or not, and their targets do not gain any benefits from light or medium armour, while heavy armour is considered to be light armour. These firearms are also equipped with bayonets, which gives the user a +1 Initiative bonus in combat.

NEW TROOP TYPES

SOLDIER

Type	Rank	CP	Initiative	Fight	Shoot	Armour	Points
Soldier	1	2	2	2	1	None	16
Weapons	Rifle with bayonet						
Attributes	None						
Options	• None						

CAPTAIN

Type	Rank	CP	Initiative	Fight	Shoot	Armour	Points
Soldier	2	2	2	3	1	None	16
Weapons	Katana and revolver						
Attributes	Commander						
Options	• None						

FACTIONS

SHINSENGUMI

The Shinsengumi were a Samurai militia loyal to the Emperor that rose to prominence in the 1860s. In reality, they spent their time fighting pro-Shogunate militia in the streets and became known as the 'Wolves of Mibu' after the suburb of Edo (now Tokyo) in which they were based. The Shinsengumi were strict adherents to the code of Bushido and merciless to their opponents.

To field a Shinsengumi Buntai in *Ronin* use the Bushi list with the following modifications:

- Only Samurai may be chosen.
- No model may wear armour.
- At least three quarters of the models must be armed with katana and wakizashi only.
- The highest ranked model may have a Revolver for +3 points.
- No Swords-for-Hire are permitted.

This same list could also be used for the pro-Shogunate opponents of the Shinsengumi.

IMPERIALIST TROOPS

The troops that fought for the Emperor in the Boshin War of 1868–69 may be represented by the Bushi list, with the following adjustments:

- At least half the models must be Soldiers (see above).
- There may be one Captain (see above) for every five Soldiers.
- No Swords-for-Hire are permitted.
- Victory Points are not gained for collecting heads.

SHOGUNATE TROOPS

Though less modern than the Imperial troops in the Boshin War, the Shogunate forces still had many European-trained soldiers. These may be represented by the Bushi list, with the following adjustments:

- No more than half of the models may be Soldiers (see above).
- There may be one Captain (see above) for every five Soldiers.
- No Swords-for-Hire are permitted.
- Victory Points are not gained for collecting heads.

The Imperialist and Shogunate Troops lists could also be used for the Satsuma Rebellion of 1877, which was the last Samurai revolt against the new government of Japan.

YAKUZA

During the late Edo period the criminal gangs that would become known as Yakuza were first heard of. These may be represented by the Bandits list, with the following adjustments:

- No model may wear armour.
- The highest ranked model may have a revolver for +3 points.

SOHEI

The existing Sohei list may be used.

KORYU

The existing Koryu list may be used.

FURTHER READING

RECOMMENDED READING

The following Osprey titles will provide all the information you need on the Sengoku Jidai period.

- *Ashigaru 1467–1649* (Warrior 29) – Stephen Turnbull
- *Japanese Warrior Monks AD 949–1603* (Warrior 70) – Stephen Turnbull
- *Samurai Armies 1467–1649* (Battle Orders 36) – Stephen Turnbull
- *The Samurai Invasion of Korea 1592–98* (Campaign 198) – Stephen Turnbull
- *Samurai 1550–1600* (Warrior 7) – Stephen Turnbull
- *Ninja AD 1460–1650* (Warrior 64) – Stephen Turnbull

FILMS

The late, great Akira Kurosawa was one of the greatest film makers of all time, and his work heavily influenced these rules. Kurosawa's Samurai films are as follows:

- *Rashomon*
- *Seven Samurai*
- *Throne of Blood*
- *The Hidden Fortress*
- *Yojimbo*
- *Sanjuro*
- *Kagemusha*
- *Ran*

Other films worth watching include:

- *Zatoichi*
- *Twilight Samurai*
- *13 Assassins*
- *47 Ronin*

COUNTERS SHEET

STUNNED

LIGHT WOUND

GRIEVOUS WOUND

SLAIN

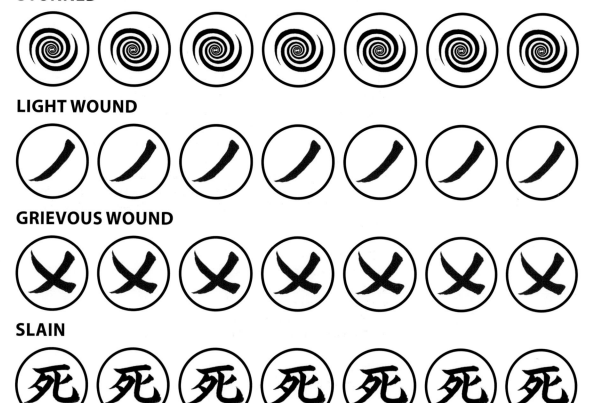

REFERENCE SHEET

TURN SEQUENCE

1. Priority Phase
2. Move Phase
3. Combat Phase
4. Action Phase
5. End Phase

PRIORITY PHASE

1. Determine Priority
2. Test Morale

TEST MORALE

Check when:

- The Buntai's Morale is currently Wavering
- At least 25% of the starting strength of the Buntai suffered a Critical wound in the previous turn (for example, if a Buntai that started the game with 10 models loses 3 to critical wounds in any one turn, it must test the following turn).
- The Leader of the Buntai suffers a Critical wound.

Roll 2d6 +/- modifiers (A natural roll of 2 is always a success and a natural roll of 12 is always a failure):

- The Buntai is at less than half strength: +1
- The Buntai's Morale is currently Wavering: +1
- The Buntai has at least one model with the Commander ability: -1
- The Buntai has a banner: you may choose to reroll the Morale Test

If the result is equal to or less than the Buntai's Morale Rating:

- If the Buntai's Morale is currently Steady, then nothing will happen
- If the Buntai's Morale is currently Wavering, it will change to Steady

If the result exceeds the Buntai's Morale Rating:

- If the Buntai's Morale is currently Steady, it will change to Wavering
- If the Buntai's Morale is currently Wavering, it will change to Routing

Once a Buntai's Morale changes to Routing, it will remain so for the rest of the game.

MOVE PHASE

- Models may move or use a missile weapon
- Normal move = 6"
- Run = up to 9" (may not engage) if it does not pass within 1" of an enemy model during any part of its movement
- Move halved if Stunned, Grievously wounded, Encumbered, or moving through Difficult Terrain
- May Withdraw 2" if in base-to-base combat with an enemy
- Mounted models move 12" or Gallop 18" or make Ride-by-attack (9" now, 9" in Action Phase)

SHOOTING ATTACKS

- Attacker Rolls 2d6 +/- modifiers
- Defender adds modifiers to a base of 6

Modifiers to Shooting Attack Roll	
Target is less than 6" away	+1
Target is 12–24" away	-1
Target is 24–36" away	-2 (-3 if shooting with a teppo)
Target is more than 36" away	-3 (-4 if shooting with a teppo)
Target is engaged in combat	-1 (plus see special rules for shooting into combat)
Shooting Model made a normal move this turn	-1
Shooting Model made a Run or Gallop move this turn	-2
Shooting Model previously fired this turn	-1
Shooting Model is shooting in the Move Phase	-1
Shooting Model has a Grievous wound	-1
All modifiers are cumulative.	

Modifiers to Shooting Defence Score	
Target has light armour	+1
Target has medium armour	+2
Target has heavy armour	+3
Target is in Light cover	+1
Target is in Heavy cover	+2
All modifiers are cumulative.	

Weapon	Maximum Range	Wound Modifier	Special
Shuriken (throwing star)	6"	-2	There is no penalty for moving and using a shuriken.
Teppo (arquebus)	48"	Special	The teppo, or arquebus, must be reloaded before it can be fired again (see Action Phase, below). Whenever a teppo is fired, it is helpful to place a small ball of cotton wool or similar next to the model to signify this. A teppo is inaccurate at long ranges, and so all shots of more than 24" incur an additional -1 penalty. Models that are fired at with a teppo do not gain any benefits from light or medium armour, and heavy armour is considered to be light armour.
Yumi (bow)	48"		

COMBAT PHASE

COMBAT PROCESS

1. Draw counters equal to Combat Pool
2. Determine Initiative
3. First model attacks – rolls 2d6 (3d6 if Enhanceed) and adds Fight and any modifiers. Defender rolls 1d6 (2d6 if Enhanceed) and adds modifiers

Weapon	Initiative Modifier	Attack Roll Modifier	Special
Katana (sword)			
Wakizashi (short sword)	-1		
Nodachi (two-handed sword)	-1	+1	
Tanto (dagger)	-1	-1	
Naginata (halberd	+1	+1	
Yari (spear)	+2		+1 Attack Roll Modifier if mounted and making a ride-by attack.
Nagae-yari (pike)	+3/-2		This weapon provides a +3 Initiative bonus in the first round of combat. However, if this same combat continues for another turn, the wielder suffers a -2 Initiative penalty for each subsequent turn.
Jo (short staff)	+1		
Bo (quarterstaff)			
Tetsubo (long club)	-1	+1	
Kasurigama (sickle and chain)	+1/-		This weapon provides a +1 Initiative bonus in the first round of combat and +1 to any Subdue attempt.
Weaponless	-1	-1	This represents fighting without a weapon, using punches, kicks and grappling techniques. Such attacks suffer an additional -1 penalty when directed against models equipped with heavy armour.
Improvised weapon	-1		

Modifiers to Defence Roll	
Target has light armour	+1
Target has medium armour	+2
Target has heavy armour	+3
Target is engaged by 3 or more enemy models	-1

ENHANCING

- When you Enhance an Initiative Roll, you roll 2 dice and discard 1.
- When you Enhance an Attack Roll, you roll 3 dice and discard 1.
- When you Enhance a Defence Roll, you roll 2 dice and keep both.

WOUNDS

Wound Score	Result	Effect
1	Stunned	-1 to Initiative
2–3	Light wound	-1 to Initiative, -1 to Fight
4–5	Grievous wound	-2 to Initiative, -1 to Fight, -1 to Combat Pool, -1 to Shoot
6	Critical wound	This model has been killed

ACTION PHASE

Models may:

- Use a missile weapon
- Reload a teppo
- Loot a body or collect a head
- Pick up an object
- Mount or dismount
- Rest

END PHASE

REMOVE STUNNED COUNTERS

Roll a d6 for each model that has one or more Stunned counters and apply the result shown in the table below. Apply a -1 modifier to this roll if the model is engaged in combat, and a +1 modifier if the model rested in the Action Phase.

1–2	No effect.
3–5	Remove one Stunned Counter
6	Remove up to two Stunned Counters

VICTORY CONDITIONS

Check to see if the Victory Conditions of the scenario have been met.

BUNTAI ROSTER

FACTION: **MORALE:**

NOTES:

NAME:

Type	Rank	CP	Initiative	Fight	Shoot	Armour	Points
Weapons							
Attributes							
Comments							

NAME:

Type	Rank	CP	Initiative	Fight	Shoot	Armour	Points
Weapons							
Attributes							
Comments							

NAME:

Type	Rank	CP	Initiative	Fight	Shoot	Armour	Points
Weapons							
Attributes							
Comments							

NAME:

Type	Rank	CP	Initiative	Fight	Shoot	Armour	Points
Weapons							
Attributes							
Comments							

NAME:

Type	Rank	CP	Initiative	Fight	Shoot	Armour	Points
Weapons							
Attributes							
Comments							

NAME:

Type	Rank	CP	Initiative	Fight	Shoot	Armour	Points
Weapons							
Attributes							
Comments							